LEE'S RETREAT

A History and Field Guide

*A mile-by-mile description of sites and events
associated with the final days of
Robert E. Lee's Army of Northern Virginia*

Petersburg to Appomattox, April 1865

By

Chris Calkins

Maps by Steve Stanley

Page One History Publications

Richmond, Virginia

First Edition

The artwork reproduced on the cover is by Dick Richardson. Prints are available from the artist:

Dick Richardson
PO Box 107, Route 1
Bentonville VA 22610

Modern photographs by Don Pierce and Sarah Calkins.
1930s photographs and contemporary drawings from the author's collection.
Designed by Norma Pierce.

Printed by Worth Higgins and Associates in Richmond, Virginia.

ISBN 0-9704367-0-X

"So we moved on in disorder, keeping no regular column, no regular pace. When a soldier became weary, he fell out, ate his scanty rations — if, indeed, he had any — rested, rose and resumed the march.... There were not many words spoken. An indescribable sadness weighed upon us. The men were very gentle toward each other."

— Lt. J.F.J. Caldwell, a South Carolinian

Reading the code

▼ Indicates driving instructions.

 Tour route on maps.

 Wayside indicator in text. Interpretation on signs and by radio messages is provided at stops where you see this sign.

 Lee's Retreat Wayside on maps.

 Confederate troops.

 Union troops.

Introduction

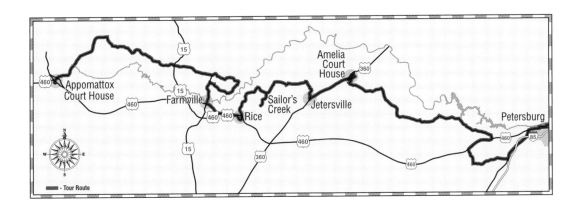

$\mathcal{T}$he Lee's Retreat driving tour that this book follows was developed in the early 1990s by the counties, cities and towns along the roads used by Union and Confederate armies April 2-9, 1865.

Historically, marching soldiers filled the roads from Richmond and Petersburg to Appomattox. The route outlined on the tour and in this book follows no particular unit of either army. Instead, it catches up with many different elements; "connecting the dots" of significant actions along the way while directing travelers through largely unspoiled landscapes on roads the soldiers used.

Chris Calkins, historian at the Petersburg National Battlefield, is largely responsible for organizing the historical fabric on the tour. He is the author of several books on the Appomattox Campaign including two tour guides more detailed than this one. "From Petersburg to Appomattox: A tour guide to the routes of Lee's withdrawal and Grant's pursuit, April 2-9, 1865" and "Thirty-Six Hours Before Appomattox: April 6 and 7, 1865" are available at the National Park Service visitor centers at Petersburg and Appomattox.

This book is intended as a companion for those driving the official Lee's Retreat driving tour, but it should prove useful to anyone trying to understand the last days of the Army of Northern Virginia.

When you take the tour, follow the "trailblazer signs" located at strategic intersections. Radio messages are broadcast at the official way-sides. Tune your radio to AM 1610 (AM 1600 near Petersburg and Appomattox). The broadcasts are limited in range. You must stop at the waysides to hear them. Recordings of the radio messages are available on cassette tape and compact disc. They are reliable, inexpensive and cued to the stops.

Allow at least six hours for the tour. That covers driving and time to listen to the recorded messages and read the waysides. If you are prone to exploring, take all day. This tour covers more than 140 miles, using mostly rural roads. All are paved, but you should use caution. Opportunities for fuel, food and restroom stops are scarce outside Petersburg, Amelia, Farmville and Appomattox.

▼ A word about the mileage

Few, if any, of you will want to follow this tour from mile 0.0 to mile 141.5 using exact odometer readings. We expect most people to explore Pamplin Park, for instance; take time to investigate Farmville, and break off the route for lunch. The mileposts indicated in this book are intended to give relative distances between points.

▼ For more information

- On the route of Lee's Retreat driving tour, call 800-6-RETREAT.

- On Virginia Civil War Trails, call 888-CIVILWAR.

- On news of sites and events related to Civil War travel in the mid-Atlantic, see www.civilwartraveler.com

Contents

Note: Many of these sites are on private property. Please do not trespass.

Prelude

*I*n the spring of 1864, Gen. U.S. Grant was named commander of all Union armies. He quickly set in motion events that would end nearly a year later at Appomattox Court House.

At Grant's direction, Union troops surged into the Wilderness west of Fredericksburg, opening a two-month slugfest with the outnumbered but still dangerous Confederate Army of Northern Virginia commanded by Gen. Robert E. Lee.

The fighting in the Wilderness May 5–6, 1864, began a series of bloody battles as Grant smashed south toward Richmond. The armies fought savagely at Spotsylvania Court House, North Anna and Cold Harbor and skirmished in forgotten fields and country crossroads.

After a costly stalemate just outside Richmond at Cold Harbor in early June, Grant changed course, crossing the James River and taking aim at Petersburg, an important rail and road junction critical to the Confederate capital and Lee's army.

Union soldiers attacked the lightly held defenses east of Petersburg in mid-June and narrowly missed capturing the city. Following those first attacks, the two armies settled into a siege that would continue for nearly 10 months.

During the rest of 1864 and early in 1865, the Union army gradually put a stranglehold on Petersburg, cutting off road and rail supply routes to the city one by one. By March 1865 the last reliable outside supply line left to the Confederates in Petersburg was the South Side Railroad that ran west through Farmville and Appomattox, then on to

Lynchburg with connections south.

Lee stretched his threadbare army west of the city to protect the line, but he was running out of soldiers. Union attacks April 1, 1865, at the western end of the Confederate defenses at Five Forks finally doomed the South Side Railroad and the Confederate occupation of Petersburg.

The battle at Five Forks, sometimes referred to as the "Waterloo of the Confederacy," and the general attack against the entire Petersburg line the next day forced Lee to evacuate Petersburg and march into an uncertain future.

Lee hoped to move his army south into North Carolina, joining other Confederates still in the field there. But the fast-moving Union army cut him off at every turn, eventually forcing the Army of Northern Virginia into an inescapable situation at Appomattox Court House.

The story of the last march of Lee's fabled Army of Northern Virginia still lingers in American memory. The shadows of the event remain visible on the landscape today.

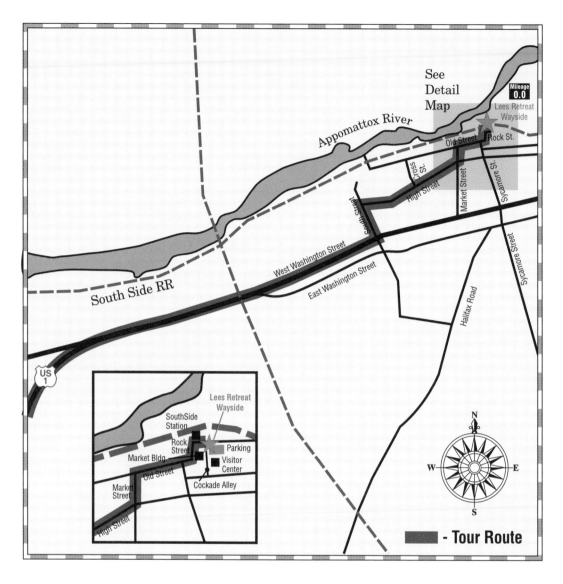

Mileage 0.0

See Detail Map

Appomattox River

Lees Retreat Wayside

Old Street | Rock St.

Cross St.

High Street

Market Street

Sycamore St.

South Street

South Side RR

West Washington Street

East Washington Street

Halifax Road

Sycamore Street

US 1

Detail Map

Lees Retreat Wayside

SouthSide Station

Rock Street

Parking

Market Bldg.

Visitor Center

Old Street

Market Street

Cockade Alley

High Street

N
W E
S

▬ - **Tour Route**

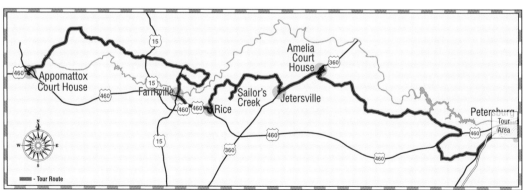

15

Amelia Court House

460

Appomattox Court House

460

Farmville

15

Sailor's Creek

Jetersville

360

460

460

Rice

Petersburg

Tour Area

360

620

460

460

15

460

N
W E
S

▬ - Tour Route

I. Petersburg

▼ We suggest reading through this entire chapter before leaving
the first stop. The sites roll by quickly in Petersburg allowing too
little time for reading as you pass by.

At the time of the Civil War, this city of 18,000 (second largest in Virginia) was a bustling commercial center linked to all points of the compass via five railroads and nine wagon roads. In this "modern" city, Petersburg citizens enjoyed gas-lit cobble-stone streets and running water in many parts of town. Cotton and flour mills lined the Appomattox Riverfront; the tobacco industry, railroad shops and iron works were major employers.

In the spring and early summer of 1864 — as Gen. U.S. Grant gobbled up territory north of Richmond and Union armies cut transportation arteries from the west — Petersburg became the most important supply center for the Confederate capital 23 miles north in Richmond and for Robert E. Lee's Army of Northern Virginia. Many buildings associated with the Civil War survive. Check at the Petersburg visitor center for more information.

From I-95, exit at Washington Street in Petersburg. Follow signs to the Petersburg Visitor Center. The tour's first stop is nearby.

Mile 0.0 South Side Railroad Station

Wayside signs are located in the public parking lot north of the visitor center at the corner of River Street and Cockade Alley.

This original passenger and freight station, the oldest standing in Virginia, was built in 1854. The rail line ran 123 miles west to Lynchburg, and 10 miles east to City Point (now in Hopewell).

Radio message at AM1610.

During the siege, an artillery shell crashed through the roof of the western freight wing and into a roof support beam. This damage was later braced and can be seen today.

South Side Station

After the Civil War, former Confederate Gen. William Mahone was president of a railroad that succeeded the South Side and located his office in the upper-floor, right-front window of this building. In 1993 a tornado severely damaged the station, destroying the east freight wing (right side).

For further information on Petersburg area attractions and the Lee's Retreat Driving Tour, stop by the city's visitor center in the McIlwayne House, an antebellum home moved to this location. During the war, grocery stores and markets occupied the site of the current building.

▼ **Drive away from the station (turn left on Rock Street), and note the octagonal building immediately on your left.**

For more information on Petersburg, call 800-368-3595.

The octagonal market building you see today was built in 1879. It is the third market on this site. The second structure suffered from the Federal bombardment during the siege because of its close proximity to the railroad station and bridges over the nearby Appomattox River.

Charles Campbell, a local historian and diarist, wrote on July 13, 1864:

> "Paid at the new market for eggs $6.00 – 1 qt. blackberries $3.00 1 qt. green apples $2.00. Tomatoes pretty good ones $12 per dozen, corn roasting ears poor ones $10. Snaps [green beans] $4.00 per qt. Pretty quiet day in upper part of town: good deal of shelling in direction of Well's Found [on Old Street] & Southside depot – in forenoon: in afternoon a good deal apparently in direction of High St."

(Campbell records inflated Confederate-money prices.)

▼ **At Old Street (stop sign), turn right. Drive two blocks to the four-way stop, turn left onto Market Street. As you turn, notice the ruins of the rock building to your right.**

During the war the site was a holding prison for Northern soldiers before they were sent to more secure locations. Tradition has it that this was the site of Peter Jones Trading Post, for which Petersburg is named.

Charles Campbell wrote about visiting this prison on July 14, 1864:

"In (the) afternoon took my children and some others down to the foot of Short Market Street — near the river to see some Indian prisoners. There were 14 of them among some 300 Yankee prisoners. They were in a 3 story [building] and the lieut. in command brought down 2 of the Indians for us to look at. The children have never seen one before. They told me they were Ottawas from Michigan and belonged to a Michigan regiment [1st Michigan Sharp Shooters]: one named Louis Mark [probably John Mark of Company F]: the other Edward something, which I could not catch it being a guttural Indian word: said that they had been in the army 12 months and had been in no fights till now. One of them did not talk English very well and he had nothing to say. They were tawny with dark straight black hair, black eyes high cheek bones of taciturn disposition and very grave-looking: robust men: one took off his cap at my request that the children might see his hair. They appeared to be full blooded Indians and they said they were. I asked them how they happened to be taken prisoners which they could not explain which made the guard standing by laugh heartily. I remarked that I supposed it was an accident - something that they could not help they were dressed in Yankee uniform. The guard said that we had to fight all sorts of people. Yankees, negroes, Indians, etc. I said that all the world is against us; but our army whips the world - because our cause is just."

 Union officer, Colonel Theodore Lyman, entering the abandoned City of Petersburg on the morning of April 3, made these comments:

Federal troops enter Petersburg

"The outskirts are very poor, consisting chiefly of the houses of Negroes, who collected, with broad grins, to gaze on the triumphant Yanks; while here and there a squalid family of poor whites would lower at us from broken windows, with an air of lazy dislike. The main part of town resembles Salem [Massachusetts], very much, plus the shiftlessness and minus the Yankee thrift...here and there an entire building has been burnt, and everywhere you saw corners knocked off, and shops with all the glass shattered.

"The tobacco warehouses and stores were open and mobs and soldiers helped themselves. In the warehouses the leaf was bundled in three-pound bales. Admiral [David] Porter tied four of these to his saddle, and the President [Lincoln] and Tad took several for themselves."*

▼ Drive to the first traffic light; turn right onto High Street. Note the various styles of architecture along High Street, a 19th century residential historic district. Many of these homes suffered damage from the Union bombardment of the town.

Dodson's Tavern, 311 High St.
On right.

Miss Victoria Dodson, an occupant of the house during the siege, remembered that Lee sometimes dined here during the winter of 1864–65, probably when he was quartered up the street.

Mile 0.6 Grace Episcopal Church site
Corner of High and Cross streets; historical marker on right.

This structure was built in 1859, razed in 1959. Lee worshiped here at some point during the siege. The churchyard was used as a temporary burial ground.

Charles Campbell wrote in his diary on June 21, 1864:

"The daughter of the Rev. Mr. Gibson was buried a few days ago in Grace Church yard because of the shells falling in Blandford [cemetery], Col. Page [26th Virginia Infantry] of Wises brigade and Dr. Bellingham of Petersburg militia have been also buried there for same reason."

John Wise substantiated this:

"As we moved onward, one of our party pointed to where Colonel Page of our brigade was buried. He had been killed but a week before, and was buried near the front door of a church, within three feet of the sidewalk."

Across the street from the church site was the location of William R. Johnson & Brother [also known as James B. McCulloch's] Tobacco Factory (southwest corner of High and Lafayette streets, site).

The original factory building burned in 1884 and was replaced with the current structure. The factory was used as a temporary prison for Federal officers during the siege. Immediately after the war, it was referred to as "Camp Distribution" during the Union occupation of the town.

Diarist Campbell noted on June 17, 1864:

"Our people captured 3 or 400 prisoners. They were sent to McCulloch's factory on High Street." Later, on the 21st, he wrote "The city battalion is quartered back of Johnson's factory (on High Street near where there was a fort in early colonial times and where the British encamped in 1781)."

Mile 0.7 Lee's Headquarters, 558 High St.
On left; note the outbuilding and white porches.

Lee

Gen. Lee quartered in this house, which is altered from its original appearance, during the month of November 1864. It was owned then by William Hurt Beasley. The small structure in the yard is said to have been used as an office by the general.

Col. Walter Taylor, one of Lee's aides, wrote on Nov. 7:

"I took possession of a vacant house and had his [Lee's] room prepared, with a cheerful fire, and everything made as cozy as possible. It was entirely too pleasant for him, for he is never so uncomfortable as when comfortable. [After a brief visit to the cavalry lines with Lee] I returned to the house we had vacated, where we are now comfortably established. This is the first time we have been quartered in a house.

On Nov. 27, Taylor noted:

"While General Lee was in Richmond, I concluded to move headquarters, as a party that proposed to occupy the house as soon as we should vacate had given a gentle hint by sending to inquire 'when General Lee would leave the house.'"

Lee noted to his wife in a letter of Nov. 25:

"On arriving here [Petersburg] on the evening of the 23rd I found we had changed our camp. The house that we were occupying was wanted, indeed had been rented by a newly married couple, & they had ejected Col Taylor that day."

The general and his staff moved to the Turnbull house, "Edge Hill," on the western outskirts of Petersburg.

▼ At the traffic light at South Street, turn left and drive to the next light, West Washington Street, then turn right.

South Street was at the westernmost fringe of the city during the war; beyond was a scattering of houses amid open countryside and Confederate fortifications.

Mile 1.8 Gen. Ambrose Powell Hill's Headquarters site
On the south side (left) of the Wythe-Washington-street fork.

The Widow Knight's residence, "Indiana," was the Third Corps headquarters during the siege. Gen. Hill's family stayed in a small cottage on the property of James M. Venable, which was located across the street on the north side of Washington Street. It was from "Indiana" that Hill made his fateful ride early on April 2, 1865. He was killed later that morning.

Mile 2.5 Confederate Inner Defenses
Approximately the intersection with Mill Road

The original defenses, known as the "Dimmock Line" (named after the Confederate engineer Capt. Charles H. Dimmock), passed over this ridge, facing to the west (the direction you are traveling). Batteries 52 and 53 were astride Cox Road (the wartime Cox Road ran just south of the modern road you are on) near this point. The defenses were held by Gen. Charles Field's division, Longstreet's Corps, on April 2, 1865, during the final assault on the city. Field's division had been ordered to this position from north of the James River at Richmond to protect Petersburg's western approaches.

Mile 3.0 "Mayfield," Thomas Whitworth residence
Look for entrance on left at wood fence.

Built circa 1776, this structure originally was located on what now is the grounds of the Central State Hospital, 3/4 mile to the southwest of its present location. At some point during the siege, Gen. Mahone used the house as a headquarters (probably during his winter encampment). Federal troops of the Second and Sixth Corps occupied the original plantation on April 2–3, entrenching across the yard of the house. During the fighting on April 2 for Forts Gregg and Whitworth, Lee rode over to a bluff above Indian Town (Rohoic) Creek near the Whitworth house to witness the fighting.

▼ Stay in left lane.

Mile 3.4 "Edgehill," William Turnbull's home, site
No longer standing.

This was the last of three headquarters Lee used (Nov. 23, 1864–April 2, 1865) during the siege. Lee and his staff occupied the front four rooms during their stay. Col. Walter Taylor described how the home was obtained for the general's headquarters:

> *"The only other house available was one two miles from the city, kindly offered by the owner, Mr. Turnbull. So here we are at "Edge Hill." I am*

finely fixed in the parlor with piano, sofas, rocking-chairs, and pictures;
capital surroundings for a winter campaign. After locating the general
and my associates of the staff, I concluded that I would have to occupy one
of the miserable little back-rooms, but the gentleman of the house sug-
gested that I should take the parlor. I think that the general was pleased
with his room, and on entering mine he remarked: 'Ah! you are finely
fixed. Couldn't you find any other room?' 'No,' I replied, 'but this will
[do]. I can make myself tolerably comfortable here.' He was struck dumb
with amazement at my impudence, and soon vanished."

Lee wrote his wife, Mary, on Nov. 25:

"We have however a very good abode about 1 1/2 miles from Petersburg,
south of the Appomattox, belonging to a Mr. Turnbull, who had sent his
family off for fear of genl. Grant & his missles. It is dreadfully cold. I
wish I had a good wood to encamp in, where I could pitch my tent. But
there is none convenient. My door will not shut, so that I have a goodly
company of cats & puppies around my hearth. But I shall rectify that."

Taylor later noted the fate of the building. Describing the events of April 2,
he wrote:

"Early in the forenoon, while the telegraph-operator was working his in-
strument at headquarters, under the supervision of the staff-officer
charged with the duty of transmitting these orders, a shell came crashing
through the house, and the operator declared himself unable longer to
work his instrument. He was ordered to detach it, and as the staff-officer
and the operator emerged from the house, they with difficulty escaped
capture at the hands of the Federal infantry, which had then advanced
upon and drove away the battery of artillery which had been placed in
position around the house to assist in delaying the advance of the enemy.
The comfortable dwelling of Mr. Turnbull, occupied by General Lee as
his headquarters, and thus hastily evacuated by the rear-guard of his
military family, was soon enveloped in flames. It is to be hoped that the
fire was accidental; by General Lee it was then thought and feared to
have been by design. One of the many arguments always advanced by
him why we should not occupy a house was, that, in the event of its fall-
ing into the hands of the enemy, the very fact of its having been occupied
by him might possibly cause its destruction...."

From all indications, it appears that members of the Union Sixth Corps
burned "Edge Hill" after they carried the position the evening of April 2.

▼ **Bear left and follow Routes Business U.S. 460–1 South.**

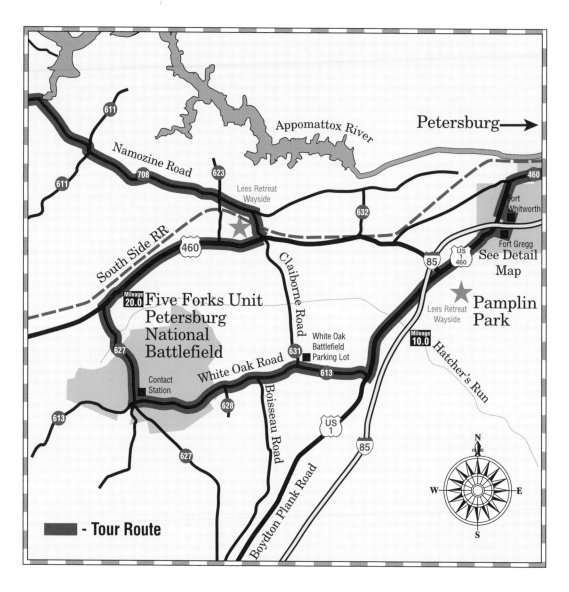

Appomattox River

Petersburg →

611

Namozine Road

708

623

611

Lees Retreat
Wayside

632

South Side RR

460

US
85

US
1
460

Fort
Whitworth

Fort Gregg

See Detail
Map

Mileage
20.0 **Five Forks Unit**
Petersburg
National
Battlefield

627

Claiborne Road

White Oak
Battlefield
Parking Lot

631

613

Lees Retreat
Wayside

Mileage
10.0

★ **Pamplin**
Park

Hatcher's Run

Contact
Station

White Oak Road

Boisseau Road

628

613

627

US
1

US
85

Boydton Plank Road

N
W E
S

- **Tour Route**

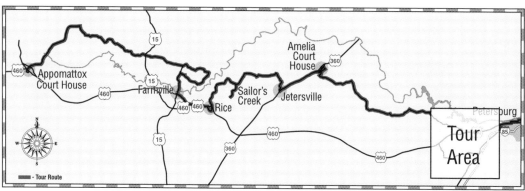

15

Amelia
Court
House

360

460 Appomattox
Court House

460

15

Farmville

460 460

Rice

Sailor's
Creek

Jetersville

360

Petersburg

85

460

15

360

460

460

Tour
Area

N
W E
S

- Tour Route

II. The Union Breakthrough
March 29–April 2, 1865

▼ Continue south on Route 1. Directions continue on next page. We suggest that you pull over and read the next few pages.

Although this section of modern road is called the Boydton Plank Road, the wartime road at this point was known as Long Ordinary Road. Cox Road, which had paralleled Washington Street, continues west here. We'll pick up the original Boydton Plank Road trace just south of the intersection with I-85 after visiting the forts.

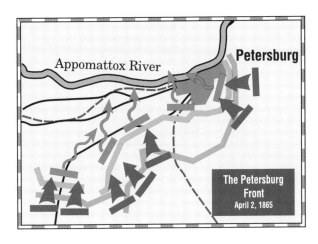

During the early spring of 1865, Union commanders moved troops west with the objective of severing the last two Confederate supply lines into Petersburg, the Boydton Plank Road (modern Route 1) and the South Side Railroad. The Confederates responded, increasing their presence in the area, attempting to protect both lines. Wet weather in March 1865 turned the roads into quagmires. The Boydton Plank Road, previously "paved" with planks, was in disrepair after hard use and was no better than the other avenues by late March.

Confederate trenches at Petersburg

Mile 4.2 Turnoff to Forts Whitworth and Gregg

▼ Turn left onto Albemarle Street then right onto Seventh Avenue. (Watch for Central State Hospital signs.)

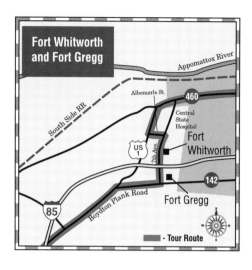

After turning onto Seventh Avenue, look to your left in a picnic area maintained by the Central State Hospital. The worn earthen mounds are all that remain Fort Whitworth.

Confederate Forts Whitworth and Gregg guarded the western approaches to Petersburg and the Boydton Plank Road corridor. On April 2, 1865, Union troops attacked these forts, resulting in bloody fighting described on interpretive markers at both sites. Lee rode from his headquarters at Edgehill to witness the battles here.

▼ Continue on Seventh Ave under I-85. Again look to your left. Fort Gregg, part of the Petersburg National Battlefield, is about 200 yards away in the middle of a field. Park in the area on the left of the road and walk across to visit.

Mile 4.9 Fort Gregg

Fort Gregg was named for the Gregg farm located here. It was built to protect the western approaches into Petersburg. It is now part of the Petersburg National Battlefield's Siege Line Tour. Directly south of the fort is the original Boydton Plank Road, which ran from the city to Boydton, the county seat of Mecklenburg County. More information on the site is available at the National Park Service visitor center.

▼ After Fort Gregg, turn right onto Old Boydton Plank Road and return to U.S. Route 1; turn left.

Mile 6.5 A.P. Hill's death site
On right, look for historical marker.

On the morning of April 2, after the Union Sixth Army Corps broke through the Confederate defenses just to the east, Confederate Third Corps commander Gen. Ambrose Powell Hill was killed while en route to the

A.P. Hill

front. The exact site of this fatal incident is about a quarter mile west of the state historical marker. It is located with a small granite shaft engraved "Where Hill Fell." If you are interested in visiting the marker, ask for a map at the Petersburg National Battlefield visitor center or at Pamplin Park.

Mile 6.7 Pamplin Historical Park and the National Museum of the Civil War Soldier
Entrance is on the left, look for wood fence. Wayside near U.S. Route 1 at entrance.

Radio AM1610.

For more on Pamplin Park: 877-PAMPLIN, www. pamplinpark.org

A battlefield park and interpretive center highlight the location of the Sixth Corps breakthrough April 2, 1865. A 19th century house in the park was a Confederate headquarters and has been restored to the time of the war with military and civilian exhibits. The National Museum of the Civil War Soldier traces the story of the common Northern and Southern soldier who fought in the Civil War. Admission charged.

▼ Return to Route 1.

Mile 7.0 Gen. Henry Heth's Headquarters
On left, gray house with decorative cast-iron porch.

Known as the Venable or Z.W. Pickerall house, it stands on the Boydton Plank Road and was used by Gen. Henry "Harry" Heth, one of Hill's division commanders. A.P. Hill and his aide, Sgt. George Tucker, were riding to this site when the Confederate corps commander was killed.

▼ At the intersection of U.S. 1 and U.S. 460 west, you will see the familiar Lee's Retreat Trailblazer sign indicating a turn. However, this tour continues on U.S. 1 for a visit to the Five Forks Battlefield.

Mile 10.1 Hatcher's Run, Burgess' Mill site

On Oct. 27, 1864, Federal forces (Second Corps under Gen. Winfield S. Hancock) attempted to cut Lee's supply line on the Boydton Plank Road south of this point. Unsuccessful in their endeavor, Federal forces fell back to their lines.

Mile 10.4 White Oak Road

▼ Turn right on Route 613, White Oak Road

Branching off from the Boydton Plank Road, Lee's main defenses eventually extended west along this road for another two miles. This area was the focus of fighting during the last days of March 1865. Union troops, moving from the Dinwiddie Court House area to your left, made several attacks just south of the Confederate trenches you will pass along this road. Confederate defenders were able to hold them off in seesaw fighting. A description of the fighting and a tour of the Confederate trenches is available at White Oak Battlefield Park (next stop).

Mile 12.2 White Oak Battlefield Park
Entrance to parking lot is off Claiborne Road on right.

This park was created by the Association for the Preservation of Civil War Sites and Dinwiddie County Parks and Recreation. Parking is located here for the walking trail along the Confederate trench system. Wayside exhibits and a brochure guide are available to help you better understand the importance of the Battle of White Oak Road, fought March 31, 1865. Along with the nearby Battle of Lewis Farm along Quaker Road (March 29) and Dinwiddie Court House (March 31), it was a preliminary action leading up to the Battle of Five Forks, four miles west of this point.

Note: Please use caution when crossing the road to the other side of the park.

▼ After visiting the park, return to White Oak Road and continue west.

Five Forks Battlefield (April 1, 1865)

A Confederate officer later referred to this battle as the "Waterloo of the Confederacy." Most of the significant areas of this critical site are now part of the Petersburg National Battlefield. Waysides in the park describe the action here April 1, 1865, as Union forces under Gen. Philip Sheridan attacked the intersection held by Confederates under Gen. George Pickett. The Union victory here collapsed Lee's right flank and opened the door to the last Confederate supply line, the South Side Railroad. A visitor contact station is open. (Note: The park plans to relocate this contact station.)

Mile 14.0 Boisseau Road intersection
On the left, originally known as Crump Road

On the afternoon of April 1, Union troopers scattered Confederate resistance, cutting the White Oak Road, preventing Confederate reinforcements from reaching Five Forks, two miles west of here.

Mile 15.2 Tranquility Lane, Route 628
On the left, originally known as Gravelly Run Church Road

Gravely Run Episcopal Church stood down this now dead-end road to the south (left). Near this structure, later to serve as a field hospital, the 12,000 men of Gen. Gouverneur Warren's Federal Fifth Corps formed for their flank attack on Five Forks. Warren began his attack around 4:15 p.m. on April 1, 1865, in conjunction with a frontal attack by Sheridan's cavalry troopers at the intersection.

Mile 15.9 National Park Service wayside, "The Angle"
On right.

Describes the Federal attack on the Confederate east flank at Five Forks.

Mile 16.6 Five Forks, visitor contact station, Petersburg National Battlefield.
Intersection of Routes 613, 627 and 645

Sheridan at Five Forks

Wayside exhibits give an overview of the action here at the Five Forks intersection on April 1, 1865. Pick up a brochure and map here.

The Confederate 3-inch rifled cannon across the road from the contact station marks the site of one of three guns belonging to Col. William Pegram's battalion. Pegram was mortally wounded during the battle.

Note: The National Park Service plans to relocate this station.

▼ Turn right on Route 627.

Mile 17.1 National Park Service wayside, "Crawford's Sweep"
On right.

Describes the success of the attack on the east flank as Union soldiers poured into the rear of the Confederate line at Five Forks.

Five Forks visitor center: 804-265-8244 www.nps.gov/ pete

Mile 17.8 Hatcher's Run
Near its headwaters

At the time of the battle, the creek was crossed at a ford here.

Mile 17.9 Shad Bake, approximate location

At the time of the Federal attack on Five Forks, Confederate Gens. George Pickett and Fitzhugh Lee, commanders in the area, were attending a shad bake near this spot. An "acoustic shadow" created by wet pine trees shielded the sound of the fighting from the party, delaying their reaction to it. Cavalry Gen. Thomas Rosser, who hosted the famous shad luncheon, wrote in later years that the location of this event was about 1,000 feet north of the run.

Mile 19.3 Route 460 intersection

Ahead of you 0.2 miles is the original line of the South Side Railroad, the supply route Pickett attempted to defend. Earlier, Lee had ordered him to "Hold Five Forks at all hazards. Protect road to Ford's Depot (ahead of you) and prevent Union forces from striking the Southside Railroad." Pickett's defeat at Five Forks settled the question. The South Side Railroad soon would be lost.

▼ Turn right, drive 4.5 miles to Route 708 (Namozine Road) turn left to the next Lee's Retreat wayside.

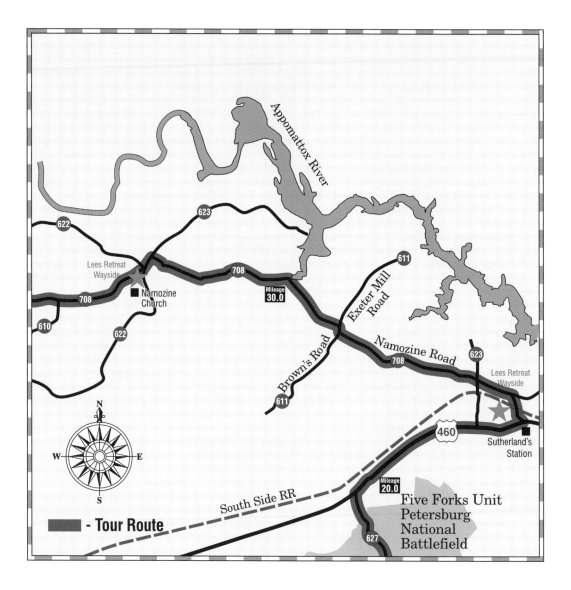

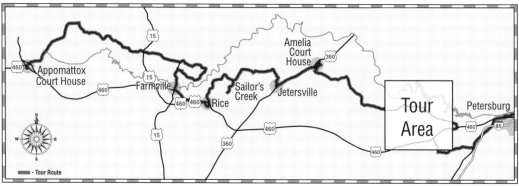

III. The Retreat: Flight from Petersburg April 2–5, 1865

▼ **Drive 4.5 miles on Route 460 to intersection with Route 708 (Namozine Road) and turn left (mile 23.8). Park in wayside.**

The Confederate defeat at Five Forks and the collapse of the Confederate right flank on April 1, 1865, doomed the South Side Railroad and made Lee's position in Petersburg untenable. The next day the Confederate commander ordered a withdrawal from his lines around Petersburg and Richmond as U.S. Grant succeeded in a full-scale attack on the Petersburg defenses.

The Confederates managed to evacuate the two cities (after hard fighting around Petersburg) late April 2 and early April 3. All the Southern columns

Union troopers pass Confederate castoffs

were ordered to unite at Amelia Court House to receive supplies expected on the Richmond and Danville Railroad. Lee's goal was to join the other major Confederate army still in the field in North Carolina under Gen. Joseph E. Johnston.

Anticipating Lee's plan, Union commanders aggressively followed the retreating Confederate column south of the Appomattox River while moving rapidly along parallel routes (roughly U.S. 460) south of Lee's retreat route to cut off any escape to the south.

Union Gen. U.S. Grant said: "We don't want to follow (Lee). We want to get ahead of him and cut him off...."

Note: The route we will follow to Amelia Court House was used by Confederate Gen. Richard Anderson's troops and Gen. Fitz Lee's cavalry. They were pursued along these roads by Sheridan's cavalry and the Fifth, Second and Sixth Union army corps. Other Union forces moved

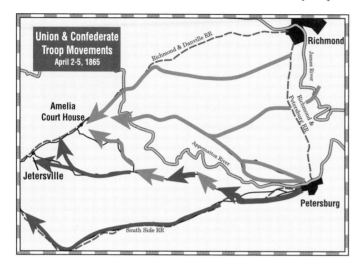

south of the retreat route along what is now the U.S. Route 460 corridor. Robert E. Lee led the majority of the Confederate army from Petersburg north of the Appomattox River toward Amelia. Other Confederates followed several routes from the Richmond area.

The weather April 2–5, 1865, was bright and beautiful, according to reports from Richmond. But the roads were still muddy and the soldiers marched on better ground alongside the mire, letting the wagons slog through in the deeply rutted roadbeds.

Lee led approximately 58,000 troops out of Petersburg and Richmond. Union strength during the retreat was 76,000.

Mile 23.9 Sutherland's and Fork Inn, the Battle of Sutherland Station
Wayside in front of Fork Inn on left.

Radio message at AM1610.

It was here in the early afternoon April 2 (about the time of the assaults

Fork Inn

on Forts Whitworth and Gregg six miles to the east) that Union troops attacked entrenched Confederates making a stand at the South Side Railroad. Federal forces, after two unsuccessful frontal assaults, broke the Southern lines with a flank attack and cut Lee's last supply line into Petersburg. That night the evacuation of the city began. The Confederate troops who fought here and others began their march west along the road you will be following to Amelia.

During the summer, and intermittently in the off season, "Historic Fork Inn" is open to the public as a museum. Battle artifacts are on display along with information on the house's use as a tavern and field hospital after the fighting. A donation is requested.

Fork Inn: 804-265-8141

▼ After the wayside, return to Route 708, turn left (away from U.S. 460). You soon will cross over the South Side Railroad.

Mile 24.6 River Road junction
Route 601

The Union Ninth Corps, coming from Petersburg, joined the pursuit at this point. The soldiers were not involved actively in the chase. Instead, they with other units spread out along the South Side Railroad to act as guards. As they did so, others adjusted the rail gauge from its 5-foot width to 4-feet-8.5-inches. This was accomplished by removing the spikes from one rail and moving it in. The adjustment was needed to accommodate Grant's U.S. military railroad rolling stock. Eventually the line would be open for use by the Federal army all the way from the supply base at City Point to about 60 miles west of Petersburg at Burkeville Junction.

Mile 25.5 Station Road intersection, Route 623
Williams' Farm camp

The road on your left leads to what was actually Sutherland water station, complete with siding. Although the battle back at the tavern generally is referred to as "Sutherland Station," it appears that the station was farther to the west.

The post-war farm structure on your right is the site of the Williams' farm where the Union Fifth Corps camped the night of April 2 after leaving the Five Forks area.

Mile 29.0 Scott's Crossroads cavalry action
Brown's Road intersection (Route 611 – South)

On the evening of April 2 following the action at Sutherland, Federal cavalry, coming from your left, found Confederate infantry under Gen. Bushrod Johnson barricaded on this ridge along the road, facing left. The

Union troopers made three unsuccessful charges against the Southern position, the last around 8 p.m. Johnson moved his men out under cover of darkness.

Mile 29.1 Exeter Mill Road (Route 611 – North)

Pickett, following his escape from the Five Forks battlefield April 1, moved his division on this road (from your left, crossing in front of you) in an attempt to cross the Appomattox River a short distance to your right and join Lee's troops on the north side. A ferry was found at Exeter Mills, but that method of crossing consumed too much time and the river was too deep to ford. Only some of Pickett's troops were able to cross. The rest of Pickett's men moved up the southern bank of the river another 15 miles until they reached the Bevil's Bridge Road, which they followed into Amelia.

Mile 30.8 Namozine Creek — rearguard action

About 11 p.m. April 2, Bushrod Johnson moved his Confederate column west over the 50-foot-wide Namozine Creek and destroyed the bridge. By 2 a.m. the Confederate troops were safely across. A cavalry rearguard and a regiment of infantry were left at the creek crossing. The Union pursuit was led by 26-year-old Gen. George A. Custer's cavalry division. Finding Confederates holding the creek crossing, Union horsemen prepared to attack. Passing upstream (to your left) some distance, they were able to flank the Confederate position and force them to retreat. The Federals now could safely ford this creek and remove felled trees and other obstructions the Southerners had placed in the road.

Mile 34.3 Namozine Church Battlefield
Approximately at intersection of Route 623 in the vicinity of the Namozine General Store

The Confederates made no more major rearguard stands until reaching this area. The Southerners did attempt to slow the movement of the Union cavalry by dropping trees and piling fence rails in the road here. The retreating Confederates set fire to fences and woods, exploding artillery ammunition they had tossed away on the side of the road. The explosion of these shells could be heard as the Union cavalry rode in pursuit. Intermixed with the discarded shells were a number of disabled caissons and wagons, along with arms, accoutrements, blankets, clothing and cartridges.

The 8th New York Cavalry led Custer's advance up Namozine Road as they approached the church April 3. They found a part of Gen. W.H.F. "Rooney" Lee's division. The Federals formed to attack in the fields on both sides of the road in this area.

Namozine Presbyterian Church, a small, rural, frame building measuring 24 by 35 feet, was built in 1847 and had a seating capacity of 75 in its plainly furnished interior. It retains an upper L-shaped gallery for the slaves who accompanied their owners to ser-

vices. The exterior is covered with beaded-board siding and has louvered shutters, attached by hand-forged strap hinges, that offered protection from the sun. Bloodstains are still visible on the hardwood floor, attesting to its use as a field hospital after the fighting. The building is owned and preserved by the Amelia County Historical Society whose headquarters are located at the county library in Amelia.

The church also served briefly as Confederate Gen. Richard Anderson's headquarters on the morning of April 3. Sheridan visited that evening when he reported that "up to this hour we have taken about 1,200 prisoners, mostly of A.P. Hill's corps, and all accounts report the woods filled with deserters and stragglers, principally of this corps."

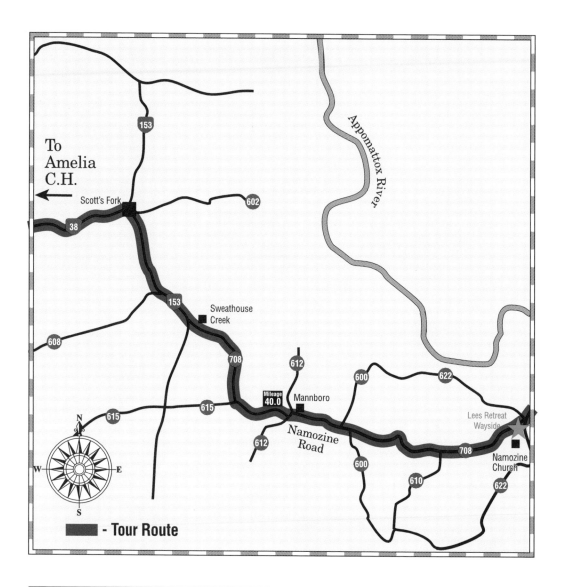

To
Amelia
C.H.

Scott's Fork

153

602

38

Appomattox River

153

Sweathouse
Creek

608

708

612

600

622

615

615

Mileage
40.0

Mannboro

Lees Retreat
Wayside

612

Namozine
Road

708

Namozine
Church

600

610

622

N
W E
S

■ - Tour Route

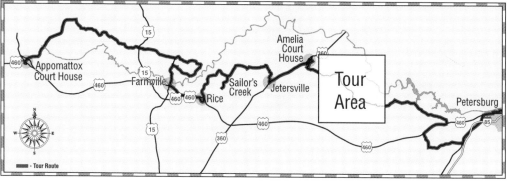

15

460

Appomattox
Court House

15

Farmville

460 460

460

Rice

Sailor's
Creek

Jetersville

Amelia
Court
House

360

**Tour
Area**

Petersburg

460

85

460

N
W E
S

360

15

■ - Tour Route

Mile 34.6 Namozine Presbyterian Church
On left. Intersection of Routes 708 and 622.

The 5th North Carolina Cavalry was posted in the churchyard, with the 2nd and 1st regiments holding the ground to the north, beyond the Namozine Road. After a series of attacks and counterattacks, the Confederate line was broken and about 350 men, 100 horses and one gun were captured. The Southern survivors scattered cross-country. Confederate Gen. Rufus Barringer was taken prisoner six miles from here. Gen. George A. Custer's brother, Tom, captured the flag of the 2nd North Carolina and received one of his two Medals of Honor on the retreat for this action (the other at Sailor's Creek).

▼ Return to Route 708.

Mile 35.2 Hiram T. Scott Farm
On right.

The antebellum structure in which the Scott family lived can be seen in the field to your right. The story-and-a-half side predates the two-story addition. This was a typical Southern family home (rather than large plantation manors), although some grand homes do exist in the area. Undoubtedly soldiers of both armies sought water and food at the Scott farm.

Mile 40.5 Mannboro
Intersection with Route 612.

Following the early morning fight at Namozine Church April 3, the Confederate column split and followed numerous roads through the Amelia County countryside including Namozine Road. The Federal pursuers stayed generally to this route, except for the cavalry. Skirmishing took place along this road until darkness.

Lt. J.F.J. Caldwell, a South Carolinian, wrote: "There was an attempt to organize the various commands, to no avail. The Confederacy was considered as 'gone up,' and every man felt it his duty, as well as his privilege, to save himself. There was no insubordination. . . but the whole left of the army. . . struggled along without strength, and almost without thought.

"So we moved on in disorder, keeping no regular column, no regular pace. When a soldier became weary, he fell out, ate his scanty rations — if, indeed, he had any — rested, rose and resumed the march.... There were not many words spoken. An indescribable sadness weighed upon us. The men were very gentle toward each other."

▼ Left on Route 612/708, then right on Route 708.

Mile 41.9 Union break-off (Route 615) toward Jetersville

Realizing that Lee was probably concentrating his army at Amelia Court House, most of the Union forces turned toward Jetersville here. By occupying Jetersville, south of Amelia on the Richmond & Danville Railroad, Union commanders knew they would cut off Lee's preferred route to the south.

Mile 44.1 Sweathouse Creek

Federal cavalry reached this point on the night of April 3 after pressing the Confederate column all day and ending with a "sharp brush" here. Bushrod Johnson's rearguard forces moved on, crossing Deep Creek farther ahead at Brown's Bridge. George Custer reported: "Here a desperate struggle took place, which gave a temporary check to our further advance."

Mile 44.4 Route 153 intersection.

▼ Turn right (north) on what then was known as Cralle's Road.

Mile 44.6 Deep Creek

Early on April 4, Union cavalry continued its pursuit of Lee's army, crossing this then flooded watercourse. The bridge was half under water. Their mission was to confirm that the Confederates indeed were marching toward Amelia Court House.

Mile 45.3 Tabernacle Church
Near Route 608 intersection.

The post-war structure on the left marks the site of a war-time church. Skirmishing along this road April 4.

Mile 45.8 Beaverpond Creek and Drummond's Mill

Buildings on your left.

The Confederates were pressed actively from Tabernacle Church to this point. The 1st Michigan Cavalry was ordered to reconnoiter beyond Beaverpond Creek toward Bevil's Bridge Road (Route 602, a half mile ahead to the right).

The original Drummond's Mill (sometimes known as Duckpond Mill) was built between 1740 and 1770 and reportedly was burned by the Federal cavalry.

Mile 47.4 Scotts Fork, Routes 153 and 38

Union cavalry found remnants of Confederate infantry covering this road to Amelia Court House. After attempting to push through to Amelia, the Union soldiers fell back to the forks below Tabernacle Church and rode toward Jetersville.

▼ **Turn left on Route 38 toward Amelia Court House (about six miles away).**

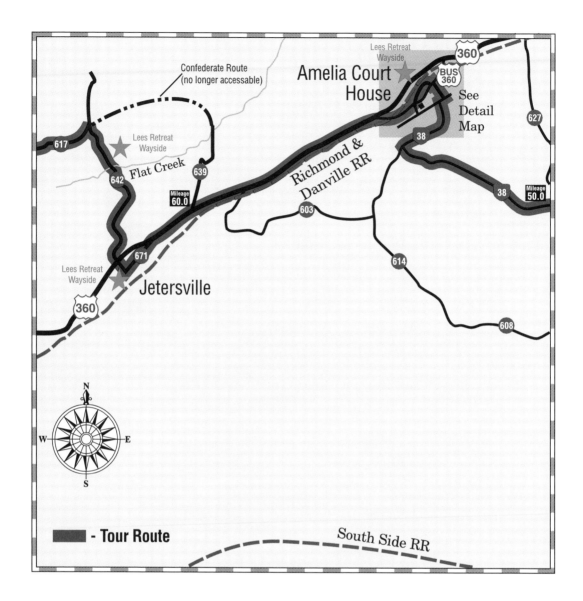

Confederate Route
(no longer accessable)

Lees Retreat Wayside

Amelia Court House

360

BUS 360

See Detail Map

627

617

Lees Retreat Wayside

Flat Creek

642

639

Richmond & Danville RR

Mileage 60.0

38

38

Mileage 50.0

603

671

614

Lees Retreat Wayside

Jetersville

360

608

N

W   E

S

■■■■ - Tour Route

South Side RR

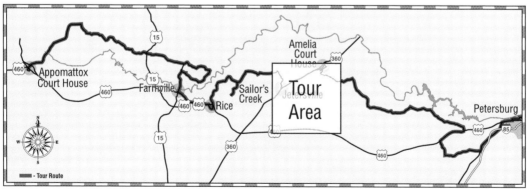

15

460

Appomattox Court House

460

15

Farmville

460 460

Rice

Sailor's Creek

Amelia Court House

360

Tour Area

Jetersville

Petersburg

460

85

N

W   E

S

15

360

460

■ - Tour Route

IV. Amelia and the Road to Sailor's Creek
April 4–6, 1865

$\mathcal{L}$ee ordered the concentration of his army at Amelia Court House principally because he expected supplies to be waiting. He had ordered them shipped from Richmond on the Richmond & Danville Railroad before the city fell April 3. Most of his columns traveling on either side of the Appomattox River and those evacuating Richmond converged here April 4–5. Lee hoped to march his united army southwest, along the Richmond & Danville, to North Carolina. But the delay waiting for supplies in Amelia allowed Union forces to catch up and cut off his route south. The Confederate army was forced west.

Weather in Richmond was reported bright and pleasant April 5 with morning showers the following day.

Mile 53.3 Five Forks (Amelia County)
Routes 38 and 614.

At Five Forks, one mile south of Amelia, the 1st Maryland (U.S.) skirmished with the 14th Virginia Cavalry April 4, which Lee had sent to scout the Avery Church Road (one of the forks). The Confederate commander actually rode out from the county seat and witnessed this small action. Union cavalry would not press their position any further.

▼ Turn right, staying on Route 38.

Mile 54.1 Ammunition dump explosion
Near Route 1002.

About two months earlier, artillery ammunition from Richmond was stockpiled at Amelia. On his arrival April 4, Lee found 96 caissons filled with ammunition, 164 boxes of artillery harness, and 200 boxes of artillery ammunition. Before the Confederates left the village, artillery units supplied their deficiencies from this stock and the balance was destroyed.

Taken to the southern outskirts of the village, the caissons were blown up and the explosion was heard for miles. The site of this incident is now a residential area in Amelia.

▼ **Turn right on Church Street, then make a quick left on Amelia Street (Route 656).**

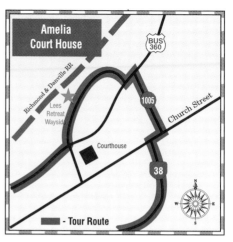

Mile 54.5 Goodes Bridge Road (Business 360)

This road led east (to your right) toward Goodes (pronounced Gude) Bridge. The majority of Lee's army crossed the swollen Appomattox River there, then marched to Amelia Court House.

▼ **Turn left on Goodes Bridge road, then a quick right onto Route 656 to the railroad tracks**

Mile 54.6 Amelia Depot: Richmond & Danville Railroad

Radio message at AM1610.

After evacuating Richmond, Confederate President Jefferson Davis and his cabinet passed down this one-track rail line April 3 heading toward Danville, 104 miles away. When Lee's army arrived the next day, it found only cars of ammunition, caissons and harness rather than the expected supply train supposedly sent from Richmond with 350,000 rations for the men. Consequently, Lee issued a proclamation to the citizens of Amelia County requesting any surplus provisions they may have available such as "meat, beef, cattle, sheep, hogs, flour, meal, and corn." At the same time he ordered 200,000 rations to be sent up the railroad from Danville.

John Eston Cook reported:

"No face wore a heavier shadow (than that of) General Lee. The failure of the supply rations completely paralyzed him. An anxious and haggard expression came to his face." The food failed to arrive by train, and Lee's call for help delivered sparse results. The Confederate army remained hungry and was forced finally to move on.

▼ Curve around to the left to Business Route 360 (Goodes Bridge Road). Do not cross tracks. Cross the street to the courthouse, a short distance ahead on the left.

Mile 54.8 Amelia Courthouse and Lampkin's Battery coehorn mortar

This county was formed in 1734, and the present courthouse building dates from 1924. It replaces one built in 1849, which was here during the Civil War.

Coehorn mortar at Amelia Court House

"[Lee] rode into Amelia Court House, a sleepy village of un-paved streets, most of the houses behind board fences over which tumbled roses or honeysuckle. Around a grassy square in the center were the courthouse and a rambling stage tavern. A row of oaks shaded the common. A railroad station was nearby."

While here, Lee camped in the yard of Francis L. Smith, a refugee from Alexandria, Va. This dwelling, referred to as a house and a tavern, no longer exists. One of Lee's artillery commanders, Gen. Edward P. Alexander, reported having a breakfast at the Smith house of "bread, waffles, eggs, chicken and butter."

A Confederate captain remembered of his commander, "Here I saw General Lee for the last time. I had never seen him look so grand and martial and handsome on horseback. He was the finest specimen of a man I ever looked at, then apparently about 60 years of age, deep brown eyes, clear skin, a well-shaped Roman nose, abundant gray hair, silky beard and mustache, well and neatly trimmed, wearing a gray coat and soft hat, his uniform buttoned up and fitting to perfection. He was a picture worth seeing....General Lee and staff rode up and rested a few minutes under the slight shade of the new leaves....presently the party moved on.... and when he disappeared it seemed as if a great light had gone out."

The Confederate iron 24-pounder coehorn mortar affixed to the rock on the courthouse lawn is an extremely rare piece of Southern-made ordnance. It was used by Capt. J.M. Lampkin's Battery and most likely saw service in Petersburg's famous Battle of the Crater. This particular piece was captured April 5 by Federal cavalry at Flat Creek (see mile 65.4).

▼ Return to Business U.S. 360 (Goodes Bridge Road). Turn left (west).

Mile 55.4 Richmond & Danville Railroad overpass

As you cross the bridge over the railroad you can view the single track of this historic military supply line connecting the two important Confederate commerce centers.

An optimistic Confederate soldier:

"We have now entered upon a new phase of the struggle, the memory of which is to endure for all ages, and to shed ever increasing lustre upon our country. Relieved from the necessity of guarding cities...with our army free to move from point to point...and where the foe will be far removed from his own base...nothing is now needed to render our triumph certain, but...our own unquenchable resolve...."

Mile 55.6

▼ Turn left on US 360 west

After leaving Amelia Court House on April 5, Lee's army generally followed this route as the soldiers headed southwest down the railroad. At some point the commanding general received word from his son "Rooney" that Federal cavalry were entrenched across their path ahead at Jetersville, blocking the Confederate troops. In reality, Union Fifth Corps infantry, who were digging in perpendicular to the railroad, reinforced Sheridan's troopers.

Lee decided not to try attacking the Union line. He felt there soon would be more enemy infantry arriving to support those in his front. His plans now changed. He ordered a night march toward Farmville, 23 miles west on the South Side Railroad. His columns now were set in motion to swing around the Federal army's left flank.

A period writer described the countryside:

*"The main roads wind through much deep and pondering forest, cross
many creeks and runs...clayey ridges, fields of wheat, tobacco and blading
corn. The [Appomattox] river itself curves often...with old trees, leaning,
tangled with grape vines, almost meeting over the stream.... There are
deep, winding, tree-roofed creeks and runs...where wood ducks nest."*

In the Southern ranks, some spirits were still high. Robert Stiles, an
artillerist, stopped by the door of a civilian while on the march. He said to
Stiles, "It's all over!" The soldier remarked, "Over, sir? It's just begun. We
are now where many of us have longed to be. Richmond gone, nothing to
take care of, footloose, and, thank God, out of those miserable lines. Now
we may get what we have wanted for months — a fair fight in an open
field. Let them come on, if they're ready, and the sooner the better."

Mile 60.3 Mount Zion Church Road (Route 639)

Most of Lee's column turned right here in their march toward Farmville.
Eventually they crossed Flat Creek on a road no longer accessible and
headed in the direction of the Amelia Sulphur Springs resort.

We will return to Lee's Army at the Amelia Springs Wayside, mile 65.7.

Mile 61.6

▼ Turn left onto Route 671 (Jetersville Road) into Jetersville.

This is the original road leading to the railroad station.

Mile 62.1 Jetersville Presbyterian Church, 1857
On left, look for board fence.

One of the few surviving original antebellum structures in the area, it is
partially hidden on your left. It is very similar to Namozine Church in
size and design.

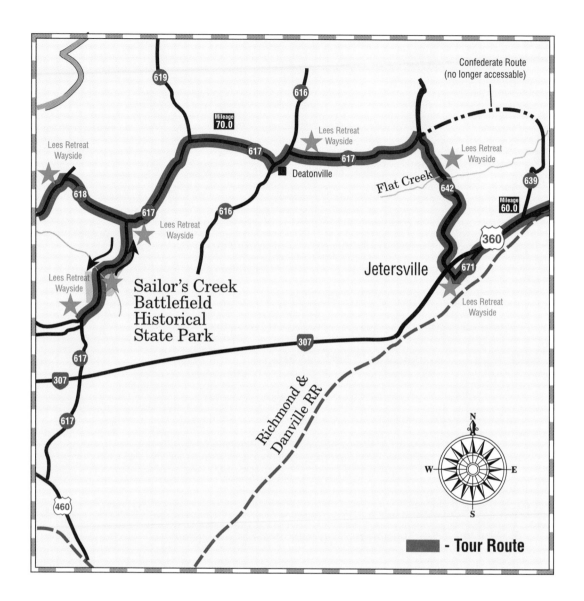

Confederate Route
(no longer accessable)

619

616

Mileage 70.0

617

Lees Retreat
Wayside

617

Lees Retreat
Wayside

Deatonville

Flat Creek

642

Lees Retreat
Wayside

639

Mileage 60.0

360

618

617

Lees Retreat
Wayside

Jetersville

671

Sailor's Creek
Battlefield
Historical
State Park

Lees Retreat
Wayside

Lees Retreat
Wayside

307

Lees Retreat
Wayside

617

307

Richmond &
Danville RR

617

460

N
W E
S

- Tour Route

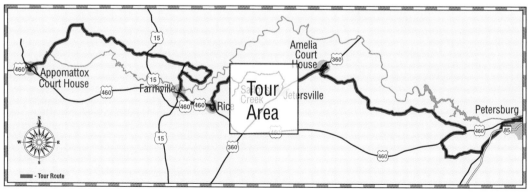

15

Amelia
Court
House

360

460

Appomattox
Court House

15

460

Farmville

Tour
Area

Jetersville

Petersburg

460 460

Rice

Sailor's
Creek

460

85

N
W E
S

15

360

460

- Tour Route

Mile 62.2 Jetersville

Wayside on right.

LEE'S RETREAT WAYSIDE

Radio message at AM1610.

A Federal cavalryman described Jetersville in 1865:

> *"A small village on the railroad of scarcely a dozen buildings, a store or two, Blacksmith shop, Post Office, and a small Railroad Depot where were found a few cars. . . . The little place wore an air of comfort and respectability.*
>
> *"[Jetersville] was an insignificant station on the railroad, comprising a half-dozen buildings all told, with nothing to boast of but an old Revolutionary Church, built in some remote period in the history of the state."*

The trench line the Federals built was located to the west of this wayside. Four miles in length, it faced northeast. The line generally paralleled Routes 658 and 640 and crossed Route 360.

A Northern newspaper reporter interviewed the Northern cavalry commander while at Jetersville about his position there. "Sheridan...ended by declaring this to be the final battle ground. (Union Gen. George) Meade's troops must be forced to certain positions during the night, and then not a man of Lee's army could escape. He was enthusiastic, positive, and not a little profane in expressing his opinions."

Later, in talking to Gen. Grant, newly arrived at Jetersville, the reporter noted the commander's words, "Lee's surely in a bad fix. He'll have to give up his line of retreat through here. But if I were in his place I think I could get away with part of the army. I suppose Lee will."

▼ **Leave the wayside, turning on Amelia Springs Road (Route 642). Cross U.S. 360.**

Mile 64.7 Jeter house, "Mill Grove"

PRIVATE PROPERTY DO NOT TRESPASS

On your right is the Jeter's residence, built around 1750. Confederate Gen. Fitz Lee used this house following the battles in the area April 5. A Southern horseman wrote:

> *"Fitz Lee came up with his division and drove the enemy*

Mill Grove, circa 1936

about two miles to their main body [in Jetersville]. At sunset the brigade went into camp at Amelia Springs, where they found a few rations of flour and bacon at a mill [Jeter's] on a creek [Flat]. Boykin joined some officers at a white house on a hillside {Jeter's}. Fitz Lee was on the porch issuing orders for the troops, and men thronged the yard, filling canteens at the well."

Northern soldiers foraged at the house late the next day and took 24 barrels of flour and some cows. They also burned the nearby mill on Flat Creek. One of the Union officers visiting the house asked the female occupants whether they were afraid with all the military activity going on around their house. One replied, "Not so long as Sheridan himself will not come." The officer replied, "Madam, I assure you Sheridan will not come this way."

The officer was none other than Sheridan.

Mile 65.4 Flat Creek

Flat Creek Bridge (1936 photograph)

On the morning of April 6, when officers of the Union Second Corps realized that Lee's column was attempting to elude the trap at Jetersville by moving west (toward Farmville) across Flat Creek at a point east of here, they immediately set out in pursuit. Union troopers skirmished with the Confederate rearguard as it pushed across the creek.

Confederate engineer Col. T.M.R. Talcott wrote of crossing of Flat Creek: "The county road bridge over the stream had given away, so that neither artillery nor wagons could cross it. General Lee...considered the situation critical enough to require his personal attention...and did not leave until he was assured that material for a new bridge was close at hand."

Mile 65.7 Amelia Springs

The resort stood a short distance to your right. Here early on April 6, Lee found his commissary general, Isaac St. John, who informed him that

LEE'S RETREAT

WAYSIDE

Radio message at AM1610.

80,000 rations would be awaiting him at Farmville.

Confederate Gen. Custis Lee's wagon train had been assaulted the day before by Union cavalry near Painville, about five miles north of here. Union troopers burned 200 wagons and captured 11 battle flags; 320 prisoners; 310 teamsters, some black; and more than 400 animals before this action ended. As the Federal horsemen returned to their lines at Jetersville, Gen. Fitzhugh Lee's Southern cavalry attacked them. A running battle took place all the way back to Amelia Springs and Flat Creek.

A Georgia soldier wrote of the day's experience: "A few miles from Amelia C.H., we passed an ice house near the road. While we are refreshing ourselves there is a sudden whipping up of teams and general hurrying among the stragglers. The Yankee cavalry are close upon us. Off we start at a double quick forgetting our sore feet. Broadus in the lead — a great bull calf of a fellow who had thrown away his gun, blankets, and everything that he could get rid of — and pretended to be half dead. When the cry of Yankees was raised, he trotted off as nimbly as it was possible for such a clumsy chap to move."

For more information: "African-Americans on Lee's Retreat, April 1865," a brochure available free at visitor centers along the driving tour.

Mile 65.9

▼ **Turn left onto Route 617 (St. James Road)**

Before you make your turn, look carefully to the right to see the old Mount Zion Church Road trace coming from Amelia Springs. We are rejoining the old road at this point and the majority of Lee's army.

Gen. James Longstreet's combined First and Third Corps led the march with its wagon train, then Gen. Richard Anderson's Corps, Gen. Richard Ewell's Reserve Corps and the main wagon train. Bringing up the rear was Gen. John Gordon's Second Corps. Union Gen. Andrew Humphreys' Second Corps pursued on this road.

A Southern soldier recalled of the wagon trains:

"The poor famished horses and mules would stop to drink when getting to a stream, which we had orders not to allow, but with poles and sticks to drive them through the water without giving them a chance to halt the column. The indifferent country bridges broke down with our artil-

lery and wagons; the half-starved mules and horses stalled in the mudholes and creeks."

Of the night movement April 5–6, a Confederate wrote:

"When dark had fairly set in, we were instructed to keep profound silence, and then put again in motion. We moved briskly and noiselessly, not a canteen being allowed to rattle. We soon came in sight of the bivouac fires of the enemy, crowded together in a large basin, as it were, below the high circle of hills on which we marched. [Probably Federal camps near Jetersville.] We went, by a wide detour, around them, and I expected that we should attack the force there encamped; but we did not. We hurried past them and bore westward. We were not halted until just before dawn."

Mile 67.0 Vaughan House hospital
On right.

The little farmhouse that sits in the field to your right was the home of Truly Vaughan during the war and is called "Bachelor's Rest." It served as a field hospital for wounded from the fight at Amelia Springs

Vaughan House

and rearguard actions on the way to Sailor's Creek. Here 170 Union soldiers were treated, along with a dozen cavalrymen and 25 Confederate soldiers. Later these men would be transported to the Depot Field Hospital at nearby Burkeville Junction.

Mile 68.9 Deatonville

On the afternoon of April 6, lead elements of Union infantry caught up with Gordon's rearguard here. Throwing up temporary breastworks, the Southerners soon were assaulted by a battle line of six Union regiments. The Union soldiers in this vicinity took some 400 prisoners along with several battle flags.

Gordon remembered the fighting this day: "On and on, hour after hour, from hilltop to hilltop, retreating, making one almost continuous shifting battle."

LEE'S RETREAT

WAYSIDE

Radio message at AM1610.

▼ Turn left on Route 616 (Genito Road) briefly.

Mile 69.3 Actual Deatonville village location

Deatonville was described as "a cluster of half-dozen brick farmhouses" in 1865. No buildings remain from the 1860s.

▼ Turn right onto Route 617 (Saylers Creek Road)

Mile 70.6 Sandy Creek action

On the high ground west of this small creek crossing, portions of Gordon's rearguard made a brief stand. Skirmish regiments of the Union Second Corps attacked at this point.

One Confederate remembered:

"By this time the command was fearfully reduced in numbers, and men were falling out continually. They were allowed to shoot from their places in the ranks pigs, chickens, or whatever of the sort came in their way, commanding officers looking on without rebuke."

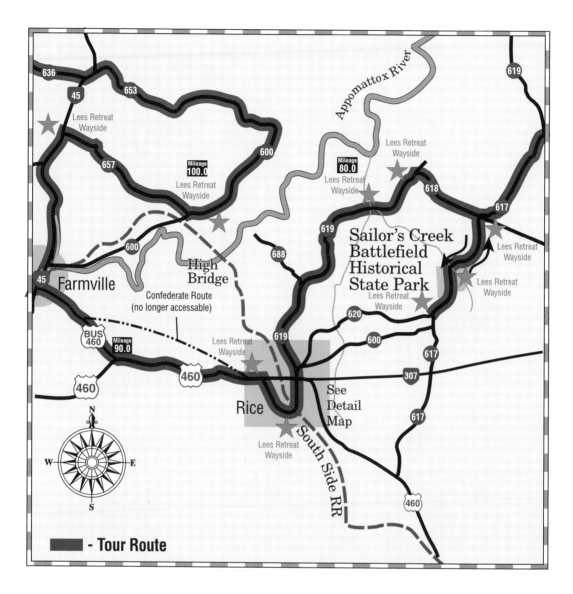

636
45
653
Lees Retreat Wayside
657
600
Appomattox River
619
Lees Retreat Wayside
Mileage 100.0
Lees Retreat Wayside
Mileage 80.0
Lees Retreat Wayside
618
617
600
High Bridge
688
619
Sailor's Creek Battlefield Historical State Park
Lees Retreat Wayside
45
Farmville
Confederate Route (no longer accessable)
620
Lees Retreat Wayside
Lees Retreat Wayside
BUS 460
Mileage 90.0
Lees Retreat Wayside
619
600
617
460
460
307
617
Rice
See Detail Map
W E N S
Lees Retreat Wayside
South Side RR
460

- Tour Route

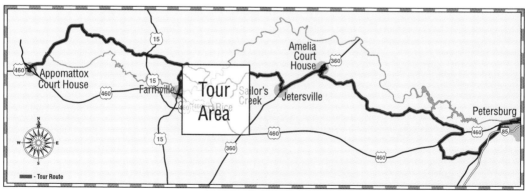

460
Appomattox Court House
15
15
Farmville
Tour Area
Sailor's Creek
Rice
Amelia Court House
360
Jetersville
Petersburg
460
85
15
360
460
460

- Tour Route

V. Death in the Valley of Little Sailor's Creek April 6, 1865

▼ **Stop at Lee's Retreat wayside at Holt's Corner. Driving directions continue on next page.**

$\mathcal{L}$ee's army was in a precarious position April 6. Union cavalry was nipping at the Confederate army's flanks and rear, striking when opportunities arose. Union infantry was closing the gap behind. As the long line of the Confederate army and its wagons approached the valley of Sailor's Creek, Lee, traveling with Longstreet's troops leading the march, crossed the creek and rode to Rice's Depot, on the South Side Railroad, six miles ahead.

The Valley of Little Sailor's Creek (1936)

After that group passed in the morning, Federal cavalry attacked at Holt's Corner and at Marshall's Crossroads. The Southern column was forced to halt, creating a gap in the middle of the Confederate army. Confederate commanders Anderson and Ewell, confronted with Union cavalry in front and two corps of Union infantry in the rear, were in trouble. Gordon, with the main Confederate wagon train, turned west at Holt's Corner, taking a route closer to the Appomattox River. Federal infantry, primarily Gen. Horatio Wright's Sixth Corps and Gen. Andrew Humphreys' Second Corps, who had followed the Confederates through Amelia County, rushed to exploit the weakness.

We'll first follow the Confederates along the main road to the Hillsman Farm section of the battlefield, cross the creek and end up at Marshall's Crossroads. Then we'll return to Holt's Corner and follow Gordon and the Confederate wagons, driving through the battlefield on the Lockett Farm.

The fighting in all three areas began late afternoon April 6.

The battles at Sailor's Creek were the most intense of Lee's Retreat and a decisive Union victory. Lee lost 7,700 men, about one-fifth of his army, during the fighting April 6.

Mile 72.6 Holt's Corner
Intersection of Routes 617 and 618; wayside on left. (Sometimes in period reports mistakenly referred to as "Hott's Corner.")

Radio message at AM1610.

This is the intersection of the Deatonville and Jamestown Roads. It was at this point that Gordon's Second Corps and the main Confederate wagon train turned right to follow a more northerly route from the rest of Lee's army. (We'll be back to this road later.)

As the lead element of the Southern line of march, Longstreet (with Lee himself) continued forward to Rice's Depot (about six miles ahead). Union cavalry saw the Confederate column moving along this ridge. Moving up Route 618 (from your left), a brigade of Union cavalry attacked Anderson's Southern infantry here. Confederate troops were forced to stop their march and dig in. This delay allowed the gap to form in the Southern column.

Two miles farther down this road (Route 617) is Marshall's crossroads. With the opening still visible in the Confederate line-of-march, another group of Northern cavalry, under Gen. George Custer, attacked. This time they would intervene in front of Anderson and Ewell, who had resumed their march. Using this hit-and-run tactic, Custer captured some Confederate artillery and forced Anderson's troops to dig in and fight again. Ewell wrote:

> *"On crossing a little stream known as Sayler's Creek [sic], I met Gen. Fitz Lee, who informed me that a large force of cavalry held the road just in front of General Anderson, and were so strongly posted that he*

had halted a short distance ahead. The trains [with Gordon] were turned into a road nearer the river, while I hurried to General Anderson's aid."

▼ Continue on Route 617.

Mile 73.5 Hillsman House

The mother and family of James Moses Hillsman occupied this simple farmhouse, built circa 1770 by Moses Overton, at the time of the battle. Capt. James Hillsman, a member of Lee's Sharpshooters, was not with the army at this time. He had been captured in May 1864 at Spotsylvania Court House and was still a prisoner.

The grounds around the building were a staging area for Union attacks against Confederate positions across the creek and became a landmark on the battlefield. By late afternoon April 6, nearly 7,000 troops from Wright's Corps prepared to attack. Ewell's 5,200 Confederates, many of them sailors, marines, heavy artillerymen and clerks from Richmond's homeguard, awaited the assault. Near the Hillsman house 20 pieces of Federal artillery supported the Union attack. The structure later was used as a hospital for both Union and Confederate casualties.

This structure and the land on both sides of the creek is part of the Sailor's Creek Battlefield Historical State Park, administered by Twin Lakes State Park in nearby Green Bay, Va. The house is open from time to time on a seasonal basis.

Mile 73.9 Little Sailor's Creek

At the time of the battle, the creek was described as "swollen beyond its banks by recent rains." When the Union battle line reached the creek during the assault on Ewell's position, "many were forced to place their guns and ammunition boxes over their shoulders and wade through the water from two to four feet deep."

LEE'S RETREAT WAYSIDE

Radio message at AM1610.

Hillsman House

For more information:
 "Thirty-six Hours Before Appomattox: April 6 and 7, 1865," a small soft-cover publication available for a nominal price at most visitor centers along the route, provides detailed information on the battles of Sailor's Creek, High Bridge, Farmville and Cumberland Church.

For information about visiting the Hillsman House, contact Twin Lakes State Park headquarters, 804-392-3435.

Much controversy remains today in historical writing as to the correct spelling of the creek name. Suffice it to say, at the time of the battle, it was written as "Little Sailor's Creek." At a later date, the spelling changed to Sayler's Creek. Saylor's and Sailer's are both incorrect when referring to the battle.

Mile 74.3 Confederate position overlook and monument
Park in lot on left.

The Confederate defensive position stretched across this ridge above the creek. In this area were the troops of Gen. Joseph Kershaw. Across the road and in the direction of the commemorative marker (follow walking path) was Gen. George Washington Custis Lee's division. Supporting them in the ravine to your left (toward the ranger residence) were Commodore John Randolph Tucker's naval brigade and Capt. John D. Simms' Marines.

A Southern officer of Kershaw's command described their situation during the battle:

"[Capt. Dwight] ran to Kershaw's forming line, which was only one man deep, with the soldiers many feet apart. Downhill, nearing the creek, the Federal infantry was massed elbow-to-elbow, two men deep, and firing rapidly. Over the heads of these men enemy cannon dropped shells from the ridge.... General Kershaw gave strict orders to hold fire until the enemy was within 50 yards. and to aim low. The lines neared, and there was a flash and a roar. The big column hesitated and then broke and fled, closely pressed. A supporting column came up in good order and drove us slowly back. The first enemy line, broken but now repaired, came in a second attack. It was like the first."

At the time of the battle this position was described as "a field of fire obstructed only by low scattered pine trees along the creek. The open ground [the Confederates] were posted on was strewn with broom sedge and a few small bushes, mostly pine."

Federal guns posted in the Hillsman yard subjected Confederates to almost 30 minute's artillery bombardment here. A Southerner, one of many who never had been in this situation, recalled:

> "[T]he enemy's fire had become very rapid and severe, being principally [of] spherical case.... The line began to suffer under the enemy's deliberate fire... the shot sometimes plowing the ground, sometimes crashing through the trees, and not infrequently striking the line, killing two or more at once."

Ewell's men had no artillery with which to reply.

Major Robert Stiles, whose men held the position near the monument, recalled:

> "My men were lying down and ordered not to expose themselves. I was walking backward and forward just back of the line, talking to them whenever that was practicable....A twenty-pounder [sic] Parrott shell struck immediately in my front, on the line, nearly severing a man in twain, and hurling him bodily over my head, his arms hanging down and his hands almost slapping me in the face as they passed."

In the last yards of the Federal approach, the field was "still as the grave," Stiles wrote. Some of the enemy officers had white handkerchiefs in their hands, and waved to Stiles, telling him to surrender. The major gave the order to fire, with results that surprised him:

> "The earth appeared to have swallowed up the first line of the Federal force in our front....The second line wavered and broke.
>
> "The revulsion was too sudden. On the instant every man in my battalion sprang to his feet and, without orders, they rushed, bare-headed and with unloaded muskets, down the slope after the retreating Federals. I tried to stop them, but in vain, although I actually got ahead of a good many of them. They simply bore me on with the flood."

But the Federal numbers were too much. A total of 3,400 Confederates were captured here, including Gens. Ewell and Custis Lee.

After the surrender of Ewell's forces at Hillsman's farm, a Southerner re-called:

> "The infantry which we had so recently repulsed came up with smiling faces. They showed no resentment, but opened their haversacks and offered to share their hard tack with us, saying, 'You Johnnies sure put up a good fight.'"

Mile 74.6 Marshall Farm

In the field on your left was the Swep Marshall farm. It was possibly near this location that Ewell was captured as he rode back to his troops after conferring with Anderson.

Mile 74.8 Marshall's Crossroads
Wayside on right.

Radio message at AM1610.

This intersection was named for one of the adjoining farms. Look south down Route 620 (your left, facing the Lee's Retreat sign). Custer's command attacked Anderson's line up this road. Confederate Gen. Henry Wise, of Pickett's division, wrote in later years of this fight:

> *"We had hardly formed and begun to move in his rear before Pickett's whole command stampeded, leaving their artillery in the enemy's hands, and they were exploding caissons in a lane in our front."*

More than 2,500 Confederates were captured here with many more scattering cross-country.

▼ Return to Holt's Corner past the Hillsman House.

Mile 77.1 Holt's Corner

▼ This time turn left on Route 618 (Jamestown Road) to follow the route of the main Confederate wagon train, pursued by the Union Second Corps.

Mile 77.8 Noble House

The building on your left is another typical antebellum dwelling in the path of the armies and undoubtedly subjected to "foraging parties" from both forces.

Mile 79.0 Christian House

The structure in the field on your right as the road bears to the left marks the location where the Union Second Corps assembled into its battle line.

Mile 79.2

▼ Left onto Route 619 at stop sign.

Mile 79.8 Lockett House

This house is private property! View from the road or wayside. Wayside on right.

LEE'S RETREAT

WAYSIDE

Radio message at AM1610.

PRIVATE PROPERTY DO NOT TRESPASS

Down the road in front of you is the valley of Sailor's Creek. The battle of Lockett's farm began in earnest on this ridge.

Lockett House "Piney Grove"

Across the road from the wayside is "Piney Grove," the James S. Lockett farmhouse. The main section was built in 1858, although the rear portion is thought to be an earlier structure dating from the 1790s. This house, too, would serve as a hospital after the fighting. The family hid in the English basement for protection.

Bullet holes are still visible in the clapboard and along the southern brick chimney. A Union soldier recalled of the fight:

> "We advanced to a White House on Sayler's Creek, where we had an engagement and I found some protection behind the house.... We had notified the occupants of the house to adjourn to the cellar; bullets came pattering against it."

An early erroneous marker in front of the house has Ewell "almost winning a great victory" against Gen. Sheridan's forces here. Besides being wishful thinking from the Confederate viewpoint, Ewell fought Wright's Sixth Corps two miles to the south at Hillsman's farm.

Mile 80.6 Double Bridges

Wayside on left.

LEE'S RETREAT

WAYSIDE

Radio message at AM1610.

If you look closely into the woods from this pullover, you can find the remains of two small cement single-lane bridges. These originally crossed the beds of Little Sailor's Creek and Big Sailor's Creek. They come together to form Sailor's Creek, which flows into the Appomattox River. The Confederate wagons and Gordon's column attempted to cross the creek here. A "broken down" bridge caused many of the wagons to bog down in this bottomland and allowed the Federal army to attack successfully.

The majority of the Northerners did not cross from the east bank of the creek but rather sent skirmishers forward. A Union soldier remembered, "The creek where we struck it was fringed with a vine that formed a perfect network. The vines were tough and would not break, and there was no way to crawl under or go over, so men cut through with jack knives."

Union Gen. Humphreys wrote of the day's activities:

"A sharp running fight...continued over a distance of fourteen miles, during which several partially entrenched positions were carried. The country was broken, wooded with dense undergrowth and swamps, alternating with open fields...for miles the road being strewn with tents, camp equipage, baggage, battery forges, limbers and wagons."

Mile 81.3 Vaughan House
Top of hill on left.

PRIVATE PROPERTY DO NOT TRESPASS

Slave quarters at Vaughan House

This abandoned country house complete with an extant slave quarters was owned by Samuel Watkins Vaughan. Tradition has it that Vaughan was with Lee's army on the retreat and was allowed to remain at his house rather than being transported to prison with the others who had surrendered in the nearby battles.

After the war, a young black man, R.R. Moton, was taught to read and write in these former slave quarters. He went on to become a nationally famous educator.

Gordon's Confederates fell back to this vicinity on the night of April 6 after escaping from the pursuing Union troops. His artillery was posted along this ridge and kept the enemy skirmishers at bay. That night Gordon sent a dispatch to Lee:

"I have been fighting heavily all day. My loss is considerable and I am still closely pressed. I fear that a portion of the train will be lost as my force is quite reduced & insufficient for its protection. So far I have been able to protect them, but without assistance can scarcely hope to do so much longer. The enemy's loss has been very heavy."

▼ Continue the tour on Route 619 (bear left).

To your right, on Jamestown Road (Route 620), was the now non-existent village of Jamestown on the Appomattox River. It once boasted a school, taverns, a warehouse, stores, a church and many homes. The port also served the Appomattox River Bateaux Line, which ran tobacco from Farmville to Petersburg.

Mile 82.3 "Sunnyside," 1858 (Overton farm)
On right.

Sunnyside

PRIVATE PROPERTY DO NOT TRESPASS

Both Union and Confederate soldiers passed in front of this house en route to High Bridge.

Mile 83.4 Route 688 (on right)

On the night of April 6, Lee ordered survivors from the fighting at Sailor's Creek to cross the Appomattox River using the South Side Railroad's High Bridge. Early the next morning, Union soldiers left the Lockett Farm battlefield and resumed their pursuit of the Confederate forces by this route. (See also High Bridge stop on the other side of the river at Mile 100.7.)

A Southern artilleryman remembered that evening,

"It was now apparent to all that we could hold out but a few hours — men and horses were utterly worn down by fatigue, loss of sleep and hunger. Thousands were leaving their commands and wandering about the devastated country in quest of food, and they had no muskets."

Note: High Bridge no longer accessible from this route.

Mile 85.5 Route 600 to Lee's Overlook (to the left)

▼ Bear right on Route 600. Cross Route 460 and continue straight ahead to Rice.

To your left of this intersection, approximately one mile down Route 600, is the high ground to which Lee rode from Rice's Depot to learn the situation at Sailor's Creek. Taking a division with him, he reached a knoll overlooking Big Sailor's Creek where he saw remnants of Anderson's Corps fleeing across the valley. Viewing the disorganized mob, he exclaimed: "My God! Has the army been dissolved?"

(Note: There is no pullover to turn around safely at this site. And you can't see anything anyway. Does not count in tour mileage.)

▼ Cross U.S. Route 460 into Rice.

Mile 85.9 Rice's Depot
Routes 735 and 600. Wayside in church parking lot on left.

Radio message at AM1610.

While Lee was out viewing the situation at Sailor's Creek, Longstreet received word that a Federal column was coming up from Burkeville Junction, basically following Route 460 from the east. To meet this threat, he entrenched in this approximate area, covering the roads to Rice's and perpendicular with the railroad. Late in the evening of April 6 advance elements of the Union Army of the James arrived on the scene. A heavy line of skirmishers was sent forward but darkness prevented full-scale fighting.

▼ Continue through Rice's on Route 600 over the old South Side Railroad tracks looping back to U.S. 460. Turn left (west) on 460.

From this point the South Side moved to the north side of the Appomattox River, crossing at High Bridge. It then swung back toward Farmville, recrossing the river on another bridge just outside of town. The bridges were built and the convoluted route was established to eliminate the steep grade locomotives would have to face if the tracks had run straight into Farmville from here.

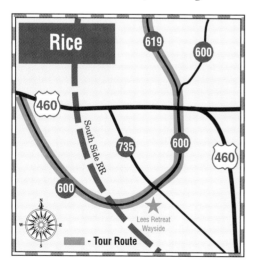

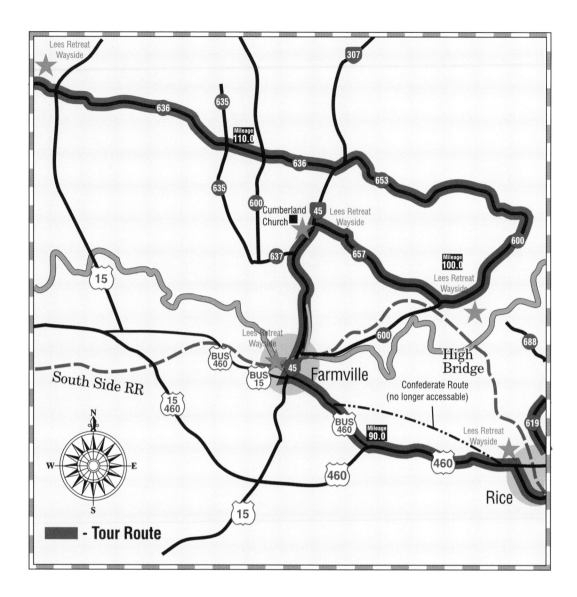

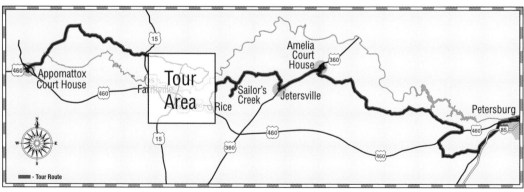

VI. Melting Away
April 7–8, 1865

Robert E. Lee's army was badly wounded, hungry and desperately tired April 7 as it limped into Farmville after its second consecutive night march. Rations were available here for the Southerners' first meal in days, but aggressive Union cavalry allowed too little time to distribute them. Lee decided to move his soldiers across the Appomattox River north of Farmville to the area around Cumberland Church. He believed he could buy some time. He ordered the Appomattox River

Lee's Army on the Retreat

bridges at High Bridge and Farmville destroyed, but the mission was only partially successful. Soon Federal troops were pouring over the Appomattox, threatening the Confederates from two directions.

Grant, in Farmville the night of April 7, sensed the end was near. He began his correspondence with Lee on the subject of surrender.

▼ Continue west on U.S 460.

Mile 87.9 Sandy River, Cavalry Battle at High Bridge
Wayside on right.

Radio message at AM1610.

Note: We're a little out of time sequence at this stop. This wayside is devoted to a cavalry battle fought early April 6, before the main battle at Sailor's Creek began and before Lee and Longstreet had arrived at Rice.

Because of the steep grades in the area, the South Side Railroad originally was intended to bypass Farmville to the south. But concerned citizens raised enough money to bring the line through the town, which meant building the High Bridge over the Appomattox, then returning to the town over the river again. Completed in 1854, it crossed the 75-foot-wide river over a valley nearly a mile wide. The wood truss structure was 2,400–2,500 feet long, about 126 feet high, and built on 21 brick piers. The railroad bridge had walkways with railings on both sides of the track for pedestrian traffic. Below the main structure was a wagon bridge, built close to the river's surface.

These two bridges, located three miles downriver from Farmville, along with the railroad and wagon bridge on the northern edge of town, were the only crossings of the Appomattox River available to the armies. Consequently, High Bridge and its adjacent wagon crossing were of major strategic importance to both sides.

Since it appeared to the Union commanders that Lee's army was heading either for Danville or Lynchburg, a force was deployed to destroy any bridges the Southern forces might use in their retreat. Realizing the importance of High Bridge, a bridge-burning sortie of about 900 Union infantry and cavalry was sent to the task early on April 6.

Confederate defenders virtually destroyed the Union attackers. The Southerners not only saved High Bridge but also captured 800 men including their brass band.

Note: Just west of this point the original road the armies followed into Farmville departs from the present-day road. The original road is no longer accessible. You will pick it up again at Mile 91.1.

Mile 88.6 Road to High Bridge, Route 603

About two miles north (right) up this now inaccessible road, and across Sandy River, is High Bridge. With the cavalry in the lead, followed by the infantry, the Federals approached from this direction. The April 6 battle was fought between here and the bridge.

A Confederate horseman, seeing the Federal prisoners after their capture, remarked, "Their coats were so new and blue and buttons so bright, and shirts so clean, that it was a wonder to look upon them by our rusty lot."

But the "rusty lot" was successful in holding off the raid long enough for Confederates to cross High Bridge the evening of April 6.

The J. Watson farmhouse "Chatham" originally stood in the field to your right at this intersection. It has been dismantled.

Mile 89.8 Business Route 460 to Farmville

▼ Exit here and head into the town of Farmville. We suggest that you pull over and read through all the Farmville stops. The sites roll by quickly, allowing too little time for reading as you pass.

Mile 91.1 Persimmon Tree Fork Road
At first stoplight at city limits.

Coming in from your right, is the old road from Rice's Depot to Farmville, which you left near Sandy River. Continue straight ahead. Notice the topography as you drop from the high ground into Farmville, situated in a low basin. This is why the rail line was rerouted over High Bridge.

Farmville info:
804-392-3939

A Confederate surgeon remembered the Southern commander entering Farmville early on April 7:

"General Lee was riding slowly along the line of inextricably tangled wagons, as if going to the rear, no one with him, as far as I can remember, and I was near enough to look into his face. He rode erect, as if incapable of fatigue, and with the same dignified mien that I had so often noted on the streets of Petersburg. From his manner no man would have discovered that which he so well knew, that his army was melting away, that his resources were exhausted."

Mile 92.4 Downtown Farmville

▼ Turn right on Main Street (Highway 45, north).

In 1865, Farmville was inhabited by about 1,500 individuals. A 1,200-bed hospital was located here, along with a repair works for army wagons and ambulances, etc.

A Confederate soldier described the streets of Farmville on April 7:

"The roads and fields were filled with stragglers. They moved looking behind them, as if they expected to be attacked.... Demoralization, panic, abandonment of all hope, appeared on every hand. Wagons were rolling along without any clear order or system. Caissons and limber-chests,

without commanding officers, seemed to be floating aimlessly upon a tide of disorganization."

Even the general officers were losing faith in the cause. Gen. Henry Wise was asked by Lee in Farmville, "What do you think of the situation?"

Wise said, "There is no situation. Nothing remains, General Lee, but to put your poor men on your poor mules and send them home in time for spring ploughing. This army is hopelessly whipped. They have already endured more than I thought flesh and blood could stand. The blood of every man who is killed from this time is on your head, General Lee."

Lee gestured impatiently. "Oh, General, don't talk so wildly. My burdens are heavy enough. What would the country think of me, if I did what you suggest?"

"Country be damned! There is no country. There has been no country, General, for a year or more. You're the country to these men. They have fought for you, without pay or clothes or care of any sort. There are still thousands of us who will die for you."

Farmville information can be found at a visitor center located on Business Route 460 just west of the Route 45 intersection.

Mile 92.5 Randolph House (Prince Edward Hotel) site

Second Street intersection. Now a parking lot on the northeast corner. The building has been destroyed. Historical marker.

Grant and his staff located their headquarters here on the evening of April 7. Local tradition has Lee staying there the night before, but this is impossible since the Confederate commander was in the saddle as he rode from Rice's Depot to Farmville on the night of April 6–7. It was from this hotel that Grant sent his first correspondence to Lee concerning the possibility of surrendering the Army of Northern Virginia. Lee was three miles north near Cumberland Church at the time. Later that evening, the Federal Sixth Corps marched through Farmville to cross the Appomattox River, and one of the general's staff officers recalled seeing the Union commander standing on the porch:

Grant

"Bonfires were lighted at the sides of the street. Men seized straw and pine knots and improvised torches. Cheers arose from throats already

hoarse with shouts of victory. Bands played, banners waved, arms were tossed high in the air and caught again. The night march had become a grand review with General Grant as the reviewing officer. Someone began singing 'John Brown's Body' and the whole corps took it up, making the streets ring."

Notice the brick building next to (north of) this lot with artillery shell damage to the bricks between the first two second-story windows. This building is one of the few mid-19th century buildings left in the business district.

A Confederate soldier wrote:

"The shells were bursting over the town, and in the street occasionally, while the good people of Farmville, in a state of great though natural alarm, were leaving with their goods forthwith. We told them we were going at once, and were not to make a fight in the town, to keep quiet in their houses, and it was not probable that they would be interfered with."

The South Side Railroad passenger depot (part of which has been incorporated into a restaurant) stood across the street from the damaged building. The original freight building once stood across the tracks to the north. Undoubtedly, this is where some of the subsistence awaiting Lee's army was stored. Railroad cars held other portions of it.

Those Confederates lucky enough to reach this point received two days' rations, including "middling meat," meal (40,000 rations of bread and 80,000 of meal were available at this point) and "dried French soup packaged in tinfoil."

Unfortunately for Lee's army, quickly pursuing Federal cavalry rode into town and forced the Southerners to abandon their issuance of supplies before everyone received what they needed. The trains were sent farther down the line to escape but were captured the next day.

Mile 92.7 Farmville River Crossings

▼ Turn left into the last Green Front Furniture parking lot. Wayside is at the far end.

LEE'S RETREAT WAYSIDE

Radio message at AM1610.

From this vantage point, you can see both the wagon and railroad bridges over the Appomattox River. These were two important strategic points. Lee hoped their destruction would delay Federal troops from crossing the river until they could bring their pontoon bridges up.

▼ Return to highway 45, turn left.

Mile 92.9 Appomattox River
Wagon and railroad bridges.

With the Union troops coming into Farmville more quickly than anticipated, Confederate troops raced to destroy these structures prematurely. A Confederate soldier, trying to cross the wagon bridge, remembered "when we reached the bridge, we discovered it to be on fire at the other end at the same moment the enemy...ran out artillery and opened fire on the road."

Earlier, Lee had ordered one of his artillery commanders, Gen. Edward Porter Alexander, to destroy these bridges.

> *"The enemy has crossed downstream at High Bridge, and will come into our route of retreat about three miles ahead of us. I want you to send some batteries to the crossroads up here [near Cumberland Church], and cover it until we're past. You must also hold these bridges until the troops are over. Destroy them when we have crossed. I leave them in your personal charge."*

Although the Confederates destroyed both the bridges at Farmville, Union troops were still able to cross the river the evening of April 7 (the Appomattox was high in the spring of 1865 from heavy rain). Union troops used the wreckage of the burned wagon bridge to get across. A 90-foot pontoon bridge was constructed the next morning.

Mile 93.2 Buffalo Lithia Springs
Building is on left at Osborne Road. [Follow signs on right to Confederate cemetery a few blocks off the road. Side trip does not count on tour mileage.]

The antebellum building in the fork of the road, known as the Elizabeth

Rosa Thackston house, was probably the location of the last meeting between Lee and his secretary of war, John C. Breckinridge, April 7. Later that evening Union Gen. Wright's Sixth Corps camped on its grounds. During the fighting in the area, a Federal artillery shell lodged into the beams of the house.

As you drive up the hill from this point, you are passing through Cumberland Heights. After falling back across the river, Confederate infantry and artillery formed a battle line along this ridge.

On one of the hilltops to your right rest the remains of those Confederates who died in the Farmville hospitals, mainly from disease rather than wounds. It is a mass grave with no individual headstones.

Mile 95.8 Cumberland Church
Wayside and church on left side of road.

LEE'S RETREAT **WAYSIDE**
Radio message at AM1610.

Established in 1754, the church was described at the time of the battle as a "rural Virginia church, painted, but without a steeple and rudely finished." Lee probably had his headquarters here the night of April 7-8. If you walk to the back of the church near its cemetery on a clear day, you can see the Blue Ridge Mountains in the distance. Lee was either in or near this church when he received Grant's first message, suggesting surrender. Lee showed the note to Longstreet, who replied: "Not yet."

Cumberland Church

Mile 96.1

▼ **Right on Route 657 (Jamestown Road) to High Bridge**

This is the western extension of the road you were following earlier past the Lockett Farm on the Sailor's Creek battlefield. The actual Cumberland Church battlefield is to your left at this intersection. The battle developed around 2 p.m. April 7, when Union soldiers, after crossing at High Bridge, encountered entrenched Confederates, who repelled them. This engagement is sometimes known as the Battle of Farmville Heights. As you follow this road, keep in mind that you are on the route (only in the reverse direction) that Confederate, then Union, soldiers came after crossing the Appomattox River at High Bridge on their way to Cumberland Church April 6–7.

Mile 99.6 View of South Side Railroad

▼ At Route 600, turn left.

As you approach your turn, look right and you can see a railroad crossing. This is the South Side Railroad as it runs into Farmville.

Please note: High Bridge is inaccessible to the public. You will be prosecuted to the fullest extent of the law for trespassing!

Mile 100.0 View of High Bridge

Look to your right across the fields as you pass the wooded area and you will begin to see the modern High Bridge structure as it crosses the river valley. During the summer, when the vegetation is out, you may have difficulty in seeing the bridge as it is painted black.

Mile 100.7 High Bridge
Wayside on right.

A Confederate soldier remembered crossing the railroad structure on the night of April 6–7:

LEE'S RETREAT WAYSIDE
Radio message at AM1610.

"We crossed a high bridge when nearing Farmville, one end of which was on fire, and a little beyond as we walked along the road I went into

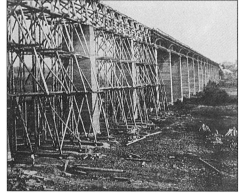

High Bridge photo showing a destroyed section being repaired after the Civil War.

such a sound sleep, marching with my musket on my shoulder, that I fell and was only awakened when my tired body struck the earth."

In the fight early April 6 for control of the bridges, a Union colonel described High Bridge:

"Nothing can more surprise one than a sudden view of this viaduct, in a country like

For more information:
"The History of High Bridge," Jo Smith's publication, is available at National Park Service bookstores and elsewhere.

Virginia, where public works are almost unknown. It is a railway bridge, nearly 2,500 feet long, over the valley of the Appomattox, and is supported by great brick piers, of which the central ones are about 140 feet high. The river itself is very narrow, perhaps 75 feet wide, but it runs in a fertile valley, a mile in width, part of which is subject to overflow."

Confederate engineers were able to burn four of the western spans (450 feet) of the High Bridge before Union troops approached, but were not so lucky with the lower wagon bridge.

Members of the 19th Maine Infantry rushed forward to the bridge and "put out the fire with water that was in their canteens together with boxes, dippers and tents left by the rebels in their retreat...so low was the bridge and so high was the water [in the river] to it."

Soon the Union troops were across the river and in pursuit of Lee's column as it approached Cumberland Church.

Mile 102.7

▼ Turn left on Cooks Road, Route 653.

You no longer are following a route that either army took in leaving the Farmville area. Because of bridge heights and weights for buses along the route, you will be making this slight detour.

Mile 107.3

▼ Turn left on Route 638.

Mile 107.6

▼ Turn left on Route 45.

Mile 107.8 Raines' Tavern site

▼ **Turn right on Route 636. This is the old Richmond-Lynchburg Stage Road, which you will be following from this point on.**

John Raines originally ran a tavern in the county seat village of Appomattox Court House before the war. During the conflict, his brick structure was sold to Wilmer McLean, who then used it as his residence. On April 9, 1865, Lee and Grant met in its parlor to discuss surrender terms.

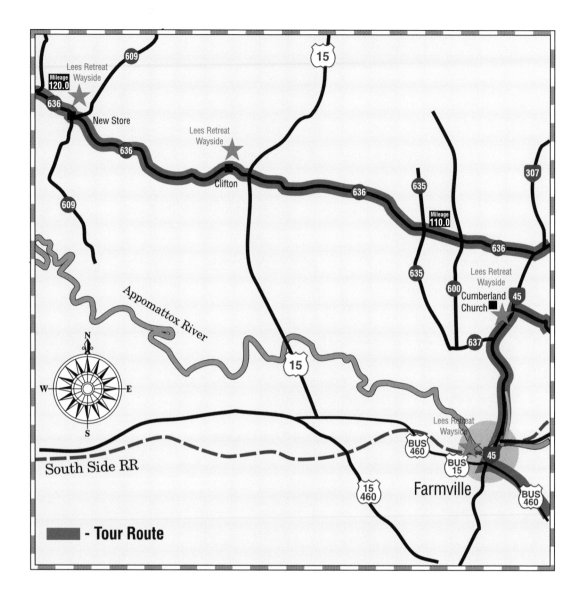

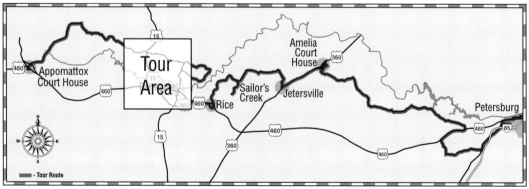

VII. The End
April 8–9, 1865

*T*he Army of Northern Virginia staggered west along the old Lynchburg Stage Road on April 8 as Lee and Grant continued their tentative correspondence that would lead to their meeting in Appomattox Court House the next day.

The weather was sunny but the nights were chilly, some soldiers reported they woke with frost on their blankets.

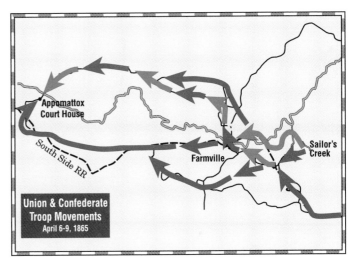

We're back on the roads used by the soldiers after the intersection with Route 635.

▼ Continue west on Route 636.

Mile 109.5 Route 600 intersection
Buckingham (or Maysville) Plank Road to the north, Piedmont Coal Mine Road to the south.

At this point, Lee, still with Longstreet's corps, crossed (left to right) heading north along the Plank Road on April 8. After traveling about three miles, they turned due west. This column will return to our route at New Store. Wright's Sixth Corps coming from Farmville pursued the Confederates along that route.

Mile 110.4 Route 635, Pleasant Valley Road
Formerly the Lynchburg Wagon Road

This is the route Gordon's Confederates followed April 8 (coming from

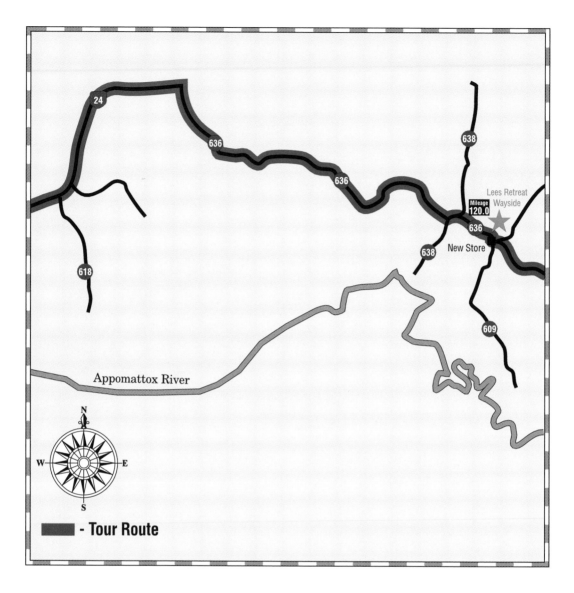

24

636

636

638

Lees Retreat
Wayside

Mileage
120.0

636

638 New Store

618

609

Appomattox River

N
W   E
S

███ - Tour Route

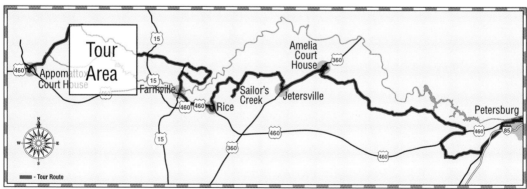

Tour
Area

15

Appomattox
Court House

460

15

Farmville

460

460

Rice

360

Sailor's
Creek

Jetersville

Amelia
Court
House

360

Petersburg

460

85

460

15

360

460

460

N
W   E
S

▬ - Tour Route

your left) after leaving the Cumberland Church area with the Union Second Corps close behind. Reaching this intersection, the troops turned west and marched in the direction that you are driving.

Confederate Gen. E.P. Alexander wrote of the night of April 7-8 as Lee's army withdrew from the Cumberland Church position:

> "It was the third consecutive night of marching, and I was at last scarcely able to keep from falling off my horse for sleep. So, with my staff, I left the column and went a quarter of a mile, or more, off to our right through old broom grass and second growth pines, by cloudy moonlight, until we found a secluded nook by an old worm fence and there we all laid down and slept for three or four hours."

Alexander assessed the Confederate situation as they moved through this country:

> "[We are in] a jug-shaped peninsula between the James River and the Appomattox — and there was but one outlet, the neck of the jug at Appomattox Court House, and to that General Grant had the shortest route."

Mile 110.9 "Lackland Well," Elam House
On left.

Union Gens. George Meade and Grant stopped here to rest as they rushed from Farmville to reach the rear of the Union forces. An observer on Meade's staff described what once had been a fine stage road now "playfully variegated with boulders, three feet high, which had inconvenienced the Rebel trains as many a burnt waggon testified."

Mile 114.6 Route 15 intersection, Sheppards

Probably named after John Sheppard who built "Clifton" just beyond.

▼ Cross Route 15.

Mile 114.7 Clifton
The building is on the left side of the road one-tenth mile ahead. The wayside is on the right.

LEE'S RETREAT
WAYSIDE
Radio message at AM1610.

Sheppard gave "Clifton" to his sister, wife of Joseph Crute, at the time of the war, since he was a broker in New York City. His office was in the smaller building west of the main house.

Grant spent the night of April 8 in this house, suffering from a migraine headache. Meade's camp was a few hundred yards from the house. Grant's staff bunked on the floor of the parlor, while the commanding general, along with Gen. Rawlins, took possession of the one bed.

Clifton

A period recollection said that the house was "deserted on our approach and most of the household effects hauled away, except for one bed in the upper chamber." Grant received a message from Lee here, not quite offering to surrender but stating: "The restoration of peace should be the sole object of all." Lee asked for a meeting.

Mile 118.3 New Store
Route 609. Wayside on right.

Radio message at AM1610.

Elements of the Confederate army, which had used different roads from Farmville, converged at this crossroads. Union soldiers nipped at their heels and others raced by a shorter route from Farmville to cut them off at Appomattox Station.

> *"Many of the men, from exhaustion, were lying prone upon the ground, only waiting for the enemy to come and pick them up, while at intervals horses and mules lying in the mud had struggled to extricate themselves until exhaustion had forced them to be still and wait for death to glaze their wildly staring eyes. And yet through all these scenes the remnant of that once invincible army still trudged on, with their faith still strong, only waiting for General Lee to say where they were to face about and fight."*

New Store, originally located just beyond this point, was a stop on the stage road. It consisted of the home of Mr. Louis D. Jones, a cobbler's shop, and a store.

Mile 120.5 Grant's turn-off to Cut Banks Ford
Route 638 on left.

After receiving Lee's note on the morning of April 9 that he wished to meet with him, Grant and staff set off for Appomattox Court House on an alternate route. They waded the Appomattox River at Cut Banks Ford then proceeded to Walker's Church (present day Hixburg). Four miles past the church, Grant received another communication from Lee. Route 638 no longer has a river crossing and is a dead-end road.

Confederates 'Halting at the Well'

Mile 121.8 Abandoned antebellum house
Just beyond Route 612 (E. Cason), right side

Another example of rural 19th century architecture along the route of Lee's retreat. By April 8, many of the soldiers were dropping out of the armies looking for food, and this is surely one the Confederates cleaned out before the "Yankees" got there.

SIDE TRIP

Mile 126.6 Richmond-Lynchburg Stage Road turn-off

Turn left just before the maintenance buildings of the Appomattox-Buckingham State Forest. There is a small sign near the old road marked Richmond Forest Road. [Side trip does not count on Route mileage.]

At this point, the original Stage Road becomes a two-mile stretch of dirt State Forest fire road — probably the best, intact section of the old road left to see. It is probably close to the byways' appearance when the armies passed through this area.

▼ Caution: Do not attempt to take this road in low-slung vehicles or after foul weather! If you choose to follow it, drive until you reach the hard-surfaced road, Route 626, turn right and follow it to Route 24. Turn left and you will pick up the "Lee's Retreat" drive again at mile 132.0.

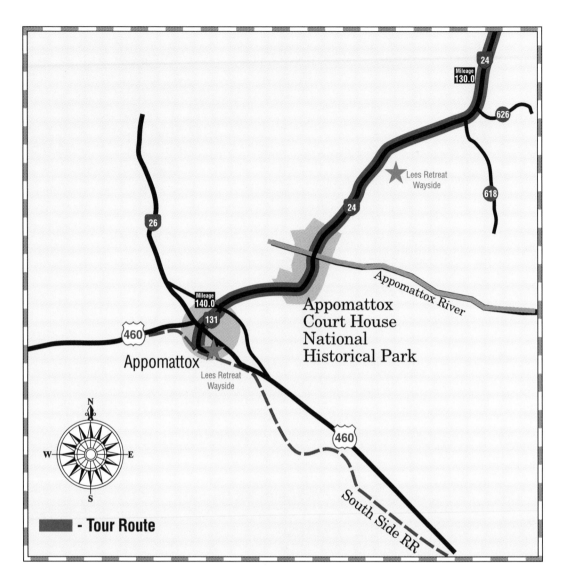

Appomattox
Court House
National
Historical Park

Appomattox River

24

626

618

Lees Retreat Wayside

Mileage
130.0

26

Mileage
140.0

131

460

Appomattox

Lees Retreat
Wayside

460

South Side RR

- Tour Route

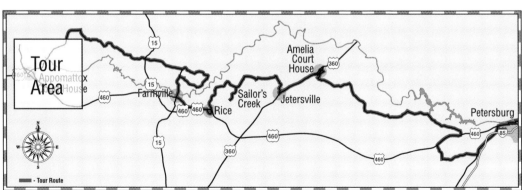

Tour
Area

Appomattox
House

15

15

460

Farmville

460

460

Rice

Sailor's
Creek

Amelia
Court
House

360

Jetersville

360

15

360

460

Petersburg

460

85

- Tour Route

Mile 128.4

▼ Turn left onto route 24.

Mile 132.0 Route 626 junction (Holliday Lake State Park Road).

Here the original Richmond-Lynchburg Stage Road comes back into present-day Route 24.

Mile 132.3 W.T. Patterson Farm

The farmhouse on your right is a Civil War period structure, which was part of a small community originally known as "Rose Bower." Just past the Route 618 junction, the old stage road veered off to your left across the field and then parallels Route 24. It passed in front of the J. Abbitt House (the rear of which can be seen from the road). From this point on the Union Sixth Corps and then the Second camped in the rear of Lee's army on April 9. You are approximately six miles from Appomattox Court House.

Mile 133.2 C. Wingfield [or L.A. Bagby on 1863 map].

The antebellum house across the field in the distance (on your left) sits on the original Stage Road.

▼ If you wish to follow a small portion of the old road, turn to your left onto Route 697. It will return you to Route 24 at mile 133.7. Does not count on tour mileage.

Mile 133.7

The picket line of the Union Second Corp was spread out in this area. They faced the rear of Lee's forces just ahead.

Mile 134.5 Lee's Rearguard, New Hope Church
Wayside on left.

Longstreet's Corps held the Confederate rear and the advanced picket trenches at this point; portions of these still exist at this site. With your back to the highway, the remains are off to your left, just in the woods. Hastily constructed to begin with, they remain no more than a foot or two high. Please preserve these by not walking on them or damaging them in any other way.

LEE'S RETREAT WAYSIDE

Radio message at AM1610.

Longstreet's second rearguard line was located just ahead in the present-day village of Vera.

Mile 136.2 Rocky Run Creek, Confederate campsite

After the surrender was completed, Lee's army moved forward from its New Hope Church positions and fell back into camp with the rest of his forces. Generally speaking, the last Southern bivouac would extend from this point along both sides of the road until you reach the Appomattox River ahead.

Appomattox Court House resident George Peers remembered the arrival of the Confederate army on April 8:

> *"[T]he fields became white with their tents, and from the bend on the Richmond pike came into view in the afternoon long lines of men bearing arms and trains of wagons."*

On the night of April 8, the final evening that the Army of Northern Virginia had to live, a Confederate recalled, "Spent a writched night. The ground was as cold as a stone — and I awoke after a disturbed sleep stiff and sore in every joint. It will be a mercy if I escape a severe sickness. Breakfast time and nothing but raw meat to eat. Trade a piece of meat for a piece of bread of equal size. Also gave another piece for a cup of flour...."

Lee rides back to camp after surrender.

Mile 136.7 Lee's headquarters site
Appomattox Court House National Historical Park wayside

Now that you have entered this National Park Service site, take the time to read the interpretive signs and walk the short trail to the site of Lee's headquarter's tent, April 8–12.

Earlier, a group of his generals had met and decided there was nothing left but for Lee to surrender. Gen. William Nelson Pendleton approached their commander, who he found resting at the base of a large pine tree. Telling him what the others felt, Lee expressed his feelings about surrender.

> *"I trust it has not come to that. We certainly have too many brave men to think of laying down our arms. They still fight with great spirit, whereas the enemy do not. And besides, if I were to initiate to General Grant that I would listen to terms, he would regard it such an evidence of weakness that he would demand unconditional surrender, and sooner than that I am resolved to die. We must all determine to die at our posts."*
>
> *"We're perfectly willing for you to decide," Pendleton said. "Every man will cheerfully die with you."*

By the time Lee reached Appomattox Court House, the military situation had become impossible for the Confederates. Union cavalry had won the race to Appomattox Station on the South Side Railroad, several miles ahead. The movement, rapidly backed up by infantry, effectively blocked the Confederates from both supplies and an escape route. When the last Confederate attacks met with rock-hard resistance early April 9, Lee had no choice but to meet with Grant.

Mile 137.4 Appomattox River crossing

This is the north branch of the river. Originating in this county, the Appomattox empties into the James River at City Point (now Hopewell), 10 miles east of Petersburg. The old ford is off to your right as you cross the river today. The Richmond-Lynchburg Stage Road, the trace of which can be seen, continues up hill into the Court House village. Continue on U.S. 24 ahead to reach the park's entrance.

Mile 138.4 Appomattox Court House National Historical Park

Right turn into visitor center parking lot. Pass by for now if you would like to visit the last stop at Appomattox Station.

The National Park is open every day except Thanksgiving, Christmas and New Year's Day. There is an entrance fee.

Appomattox Court House

At the restored village, be sure to visit the McLean House, where Lee surrendered to Grant, the Stage Road where the Confederate army laid down arms several days later, and the many other park waysides outside the village. The park visitor center is in the reconstructed courthouse building. The modern town of Appomattox is a couple of miles ahead.

Mile 140.1

▼ Drive over the U.S. 460 by-pass to the present-day town of Appomattox; turn left onto business Route 460 East at stoplight.

Mile 140.8

▼ Turn right at first light (Route 131), North Court Street.

The second Appomattox courthouse with Confederate monument (on right a few blocks after your turn) was built in 1892, after the first courthouse building burned back at the historic village. Local citizens decided to build a new one three miles away and closer to the railroad at Appomattox Station. This building and the post-war town continue to serve as the county seat. A county historical society museum is located in this complex.

▼ Bear left onto Main Street.

For more information on the Appomattox National Historical Park:
804-352-8987
www.nps.gov/apco

Appomattox information:
804-352-2621

Mile 141.5 Appomattox Station

After listening to the radio narrative, be sure to visit the 20th century train station, which features exhibits on local history and the battle that was fought nearby on the evening of April 8, 1865.

LEE'S RETREAT WAYSIDE and town Visitor Center. This is the last stop on the Lee's Retreat Driving Tour. Tune radio to AM 1600.

Recalling the final phase of the nearby fighting, a Southern trooper remembered reaching the field:

> *"Then began one of the closest artillery fights, for the numbers engaged, during the war. The guns were fought literally up to the muzzles. It was dark by this time, and at every discharge the cannon were ablaze from touchhole to mouth, and there must have been six or eight pieces at work, and the small arms of some 300 or 400 men packed in among the guns. It seemed like the very jaws of the lower regions.*
>
> *"They [Custer's cavalry] made three distinct charges, preluding always with the bugle, on the right, left and center, confusing the point of attack. Then, with a cheer, up they came. It was too dark to see anything under the shadow of the trees but a long dark line. They would get within 30 or 40 yards of the guns and then roll back. Amid the flashing and the roaring and the shouting rose the wild yell of a railroad whistle, as a train rushed almost among us, as we were fighting around the depot, sounding on the night air as if the devil himself had just come up and was about to join in what was going on."*

Appomattox Station

Officially, 28,231 members of the Army of Northern Virginia surrendered at Appomattox.

▼ If you plan to return to Petersburg via Route 460, be sure to visit the other four stops along the tour: Burkeville, Crewe, Nottoway Court House, and the Battle of Nottoway, where you will find additional interpretive exhibits.

Index to Sites